A.L. ROWSE

Matthew Arnold

POET AND PROPHET

with 24 illustrations

THAMES AND HUDSON
LONDON

To
Valerie Eliot
for herself
and in our memory
of T. S. E.

*Printed in Great Britain by
Latimer Trend & Company Ltd Plymouth*

Contents

Preface

WHAT JUSTIFICATION is there for another biography of Matthew Arnold?

In the first place, the approach to him through his mother's side – the Celtic element in him – is more revealing of the poet than that on his father's, Dr Arnold the educator. Years ago I devoted an essay to the poet's Cornish ancestry and background; in a book there is more elbow-room to do justice to this side, so important in his nature and temperament and to the making of the poet.

It has always been obvious that there was more than a contrast between this son and his father – a certain ambivalence in the poet's attitude towards his overwhelming parent: in fact, a recognizable father-complex, complete with exceptional devotion to the mother. An elementary appreciation of modern psychology throws light on a situation less apparent to the Victorian mind.

Most of all is it important to realize that, in the end, Matthew Arnold's services to education were far greater than his father's, who has received due recognition for what he achieved; the son, not. Dr Arnold gave a strong impulse to the reform of the Public Schools (in England, private bodies); but Matthew Arnold, in addition to his lifelong service to elementary education, was the foremost inspiration behind the achievement in this century of nation-wide secondary education.

These emphases contribute something new to our understanding and appreciation of Arnold and his historic life's work.

I recall with gratitude what I learned, when young, of the family story from my old acquaintance, Will Arnold-Forster, grandson of Matthew Arnold's brother; as also from the late Mrs Buckler, daughter of Arnold's old friend Theo Walrond, who introduced me to Arnold's daughter, Lady Sandhurst, and his American grandson, Arnold Whitridge, happily alive and active. I am indebted to Mary Moorman, grand-daughter of Arnold's niece, Mrs Humphry Ward, for much help in answering numerous queries about the family; and to Mary, Duchess of Roxburghe, for allowing me to reproduce Arnold's unpublished letter to her grandfather, Lord Houghton.

Trenarren,   A. L. ROWSE
All Souls day, 1975

Introduction: Arnold as Prophet

OF ALL VICTORIAN WRITERS Matthew Arnold was the one who left the most abiding mark upon English society. This may seem a tall claim, but it is not generally realized what he achieved in practical fact. His father, Dr Arnold of Rugby, has received perhaps more than his due for reforming and remaking the English Public Schools in the nineteenth century. But it was his son, more than anyone else, who inspired the whole system of secondary education – welding, re-creating the grammar schools, creating them where they did not exist – all over the country. This formed the greatest achievement in education in the twentieth century, set going by the Education Act of 1902 – fourteen years after Arnold's death – the fruition of his life's work, his campaigning and propaganda. When all is said, it was immeasurably more important for the English people as a whole than his father's for the select Public Schools, signal as that was.

And this was in addition to Matthew Arnold's life's work, his practical career, for elementary education as an inspector of the schools of the people. On top of this, a lifetime of inspired drudgery, came his incessant propaganda, in book after book, essays, articles, reports, for the education of the middle classes, the least comprehensively provided for, whom in consequence he regarded as the Philistine class *par excellence*. Their education was all the more urgent for they were constantly growing in power, in time to take over the running of the country from aristocracy and gentry.

Matthew Arnold's practical work as a school inspector, his lifelong concern with education in all its aspects, his knowledge of what was happening on the Continent from his official and private visits to France and Germany, give his social criticism more body and reality than that of any of the leading writers of his century. Moreover, what he had to say, what he urged with immense public spirit and sense of responsibility, was more constructive. No doubt the destructive criticism of such spirits as Carlyle, Dickens, Samuel Butler had its uses; that of John Stuart Mill, Ruskin, William Morris was more constructive. But what these actually constructed or called into being for the benefit of society was not to be compared with the achievement of Arnold, which he did not live to see accomplished, the dynamic impulse which he, even more than his father – almost all the Arnolds were concerned with education – had set going.

All this is hardly realized, by people in general, in the text-book histories of the nineteenth century, or in accounts of Arnold as a writer, which devote disproportionate space to his literary criticism. This is, after all, of less ultimate importance than his historic work for society or his social criticism as such. It has a certain utility, especially when it realizes its limitations – in the information it can give, and the help it can yield in interpretation. It should hardly be treated as an end in itself, when philosophic intelligences do not regard literary criticism as having an independent intellectual base of its own.[1] Arnold's much debated, and highly debatable, literary criticism is again far less important than his creative work. He was a significant poet, of permanent value, if less full and creative than Tennyson or Browning or Hardy.

There is also Arnold's personality, which stood out in the Victorian Age and is still remembered for its idiosyncrasy: everybody thought there was something un-English about it – as indeed there was. There were two marked sides to him, in some contrast, which people noticed, without perceiving what the strands were. In our time the poet Auden perceived it – without knowing why, or probing to find out – and expressed the dichotomy in his sonnet:

So he became his father . . .

[1] cf. William Righter, *Logic and Criticism.*

Dr Arnold was a dominating man, an ardent and dynamic personality; when all is said by superficial critics and detractors who wish to drag remarkable men down to their own level, he was rather a great man. Though he was not my type, people who knew him bore witness to this: his energy and force, the generosity of his mind (with some exceptions – the Oxford Movement, for example), his original stance in scholarship, his openness to Continental influences (he was first to appreciate Niebuhr's epoch-making departure in classical history). There is no knowing what more Dr Arnold might have achieved if he had had a full span of life – he was not forty-seven when he died.

His son said later, significantly, that his father was more broad-minded and free in his religious views, in theology and biblical criticism, than he could have been if he had lived later in the century. This conveys its own comment on the restrictive conventionalism, the increasing orthodoxy and humbug of the Victorian Age which the son had to confront.

Matthew Arnold's was a totally different temperament from his father's optimistic, extrovert nature. Dr Arnold was warm and genial, a trifle coarse-grained and rather rough, wholly English. His eldest son turned after the mother's side of the family and – as people noticed early on – was in some reaction to his formidable head-masterly parent. After the famous Headmaster's early death – partly indeed on account of it, for it made a great sensation, a tremor which reached as far as India, according to Hodson of Hodson's Horse – there was a veritable cult of the Doctor encouraged by disciples and pupils over the world. Rather overwhelming, it became a religious cult within the family, the light within the shrine tended by Matthew's remarkable mother, Mrs Arnold of Fox How. So, ultimately the father came to dominate the son's objectives, his practical work for society and, intellectually, his religious modernism: all that side to him. It extinguished the poetry and buried the poet.

Matthew's temperament could not be in greater contrast, refined, finicky, dandyish, cool and unenthusiastic; deeply reserved and intro-vert, really withdrawn from men, living his own inner life to himself, and silent even about that. He inhabited an inner solitariness, for all his subsequent engagement in public causes. People did not really know or understand him, as they had done the all too obvious Doctor. The son was frequently attacked for his un-Englishness – without knowing why, of course – by the imperceptive Philistines of *The Times*, who could not stand Matthew Arnold's manner or his opinions, his tantalizing refusal to subscribe to Victorian complacency about the English being on top of the world, his ridicule of their pet clichés, his contempt for their humbug; they could not forgive his aristocratic airs – he was a natural aristocrat – his persiflage and superciliousness, his never giving himself away to them.

Matthew's was a recognizably Celtic temperament – gaiety on top, a certain sparkle, an undoubted charm for those who were responsive, maddening for the clods who were not; profoundly melancholy, sceptical and pessimistic, underneath. Victorian Philistines – or Philistines at any time – could not be expected to understand it (though they might, with advantage, have tried). The two sides were at warfare within him, though people were not allowed to see the conflict – only what emerged, defined and clear, from it. Genius usually arises from some creative tension; and the two sides in Matthew's make-up were both exceptionally strong and distinguished.

Matthew was deeply devoted to his mother, and wrote to her every week of his life – his chief confidante, along with his favourite sister Jane, whom he called 'K'. The family formed an unusually tight, almost self-contained, circle pivoting upon the matriarch, Mrs Arnold of Fox How, after the Doctor's death. Dean Stanley, his pupil, adored her and later said how much Dr Arnold owed to her wisdom and tact, but for which there would have been more John Bullish confrontations – for in his earlier career the Doctor had been a very controversial character, with many enemies.

Writing to his mother from Paris in 1859, Matthew said: 'I could not but think of you in Brittany, with Cranics and Trevennecs all about me, and the peasantry with their expressive, rather mournful faces, long noses, and dark eyes, reminding me perpetually of dear Tom [his brother] and Uncle Trevenen, and utterly unlike the French' – as he himself was utterly unlike the English, he might have added.

One of the most extraordinary things about the Victorians is their unselfawareness, living as they did before the age of Freud. All his life Matthew Arnold was interested in, more than usually sympathetic to, Celtic things and themes – all the way from 'Tristram and Iseult', and *The Study of Celtic Literature*, to his later concern with Ireland. Yet he was unaware of what it was that, unconsciously, aroused and so much engaged his interest; and, though he knew Wales, he was never in Cornwall after his childhood.

It is fairly clear where the poetry came from – from his mother's side, not from Dr Arnold's. For poetry springs from the unconscious, the deeper sources of temperament and the emotions: not from the top layer of conscious cerebration, whence comes the intellectualizing, the work of the critic, literary or social. In time this side won, his father in him, over the temperamental, emotional side. Here is the personal and poetic part of my subject, as against the public man, who made a more positive, practical and constructive contribution to English society than any of the great Victorian writers who made more noise and received more acclaim. And he has lasted better than any.

CHAPTER 1

The Two Strains

SINCE IN MATTHEW ARNOLD the poet comes first, and his father won in him only later, we should begin with his mother's family. On her father's side the Penroses were a largely clerical lot, so were her mother's people the Trevenens; schoolmasters appear in both these stocks, the Penroses in particular given to versifying. The Arnolds, except for the Doctor, were not a clerical family; Matthew at one time thought he could well do with a career in the Church.

His great-grandfather, the Rev. John Penrose, was for thirty-five years vicar of St Gluvias at Penryn; dying in 1776, he was succeeded by Boswell's friend, William Johnston Temple, and his epitaph there on the walls was written in verse by Hannah More. He had two sons: the elder, another Rev. John Penrose, Matthew Arnold's grandfather. The younger, Admiral Sir Charles Vinicombe Penrose, after a career in the Navy during the Napoleonic War, when the going was good, retired to a fine Queen Anne house above the parish church of St Winnow, where he is buried by the beautiful waters of the River Fowey. This was Matt's great-uncle, with whom he stayed as a child at lovely Ethy.

The two Penrose brothers married two Trevenen sisters. These were the daughters of the Rev. John Trevenen, for many years curate of Camborne, though he lived at the country house of Rosewarne nearby. Of his sons the eldest lived as a country gentleman at the Georgian house of Bonython near the Lizard, gracefully built in silvery granite. The second son was the rector of Cardinham, on whose behalf Matt's Penrose grandfather held the rectory until Trevenen was of age to take it. Matthew Trevenen, versifier and musician, was also intended for the Church but died young. James was a brilliant

14

young sailor, backed by the celebrated Captain Wallis, discoverer of Tahiti, for the Navy. In peace-time he seconded himself to the Russian Navy and was killed, quite young, in the last action of the Russo-Swedish War in 1790, lamented in verse by his brother Matthew.

Matthew Arnold's Penrose grandfather, moving out of Cardinham, took the rectory of Perranuthno and held the curacy of Constantine from 1786 to 1802. In this last parish he occupied the old country house of Carwythenick (pronounced Crannick), which was pulled down about 1900. When one goes there today one sees only the terrace above which it stood, the formal garden gone back to grass, the drive that swept up to it from the road. On the west, a splendid range of trees, and at the back the enclosing garden walls running up sadly to a fine gateway on the brow. That is all that is left of what must have been a genteel country mansion and pretty estate. Here the youngest children were born: Mary Penrose, Matt's mother, born in 1791, and Thomas Trevenen Penrose in 1793, to become another clergyman, a school and college friend of young Thomas Arnold, whom he introduced into the bosom of the family and who married his sister Mary.

Their father had already received the offer of a living in Nottinghamshire from the West Country Duchess of Kingston – Fledborough, in the low-lying water meadows of the Trent. It was a long way from Cornwall, and a heavy tug at heart to go there, but it offered better prospects. It was some years before John Penrose brought himself to move from dear Crannick, meanwhile putting in a curate. (We see why Matthew Arnold recalls Crannick to his mother – it was her birthplace – and the Trevenens, her mother's family.)

At last the move to distant Fledborough was made in 1801, after visits to all the relations and family places in Cornwall – Bonython, Penryn, Penair, St Enoder and Ethy, where they lingered some time. When the carriage came to cross the boundary between Cornwall and Devon, Mrs Penrose (she was called Jane, the name carried on to Matt's favourite sister) got out and kissed the dust on the road, as her 'tender farewell to the land she loved'.

A year later at Fledborough she was still disconsolate and sought to console herself in verse:

Condemned to wander from my native land
When youth and all its pleasing dreams were o'er,
Sad was my heart and trembling was my hand
When last it waved adieu to Cornwall's shore . . .

But they remained in constant contact with Cornwall, the Fledborough Penroses keeping up a regular journal with their relations at
Ethy, and in later years they made several return journeys, one such
visit for a whole year, 1812–13. Meanwhile they acclimatized themselves to the strange country by the Trent, with its periodic floodings,
the higher wolds and the good cheer.

Other members of the family came to keep them company, the
younger generation grew up and brought their friends. Another
Mary Penrose, who had been the Duchess's companion, married a
local clergyman. The vicar's eldest son, yet a third Rev. John Penrose,
married Elizabeth Cartwright, who as Mrs Markham wrote the
historical bestsellers of the time. He himself was a prolific author of
books on theological and improving subjects, though he also wrote
one of more interest to us, the biographies of Admiral Penrose and
Captain Trevenen, his paternal and maternal uncles. Sister Lydia
wrote on Nottinghamshire, not Cornish, history. They were becoming deracinated.

Perhaps it was all the more a united and exceptionally happy
family that gathered round the old patriarch, John Penrose, gentle,
kindly and wise, until his death in 1829. Mary was the only one of his
daughters to marry; the rest stayed by him and kept together after
his death. His funeral service was conducted by John Keble, another
college friend of his son Trevenen, along with young Thomas
Arnold. It is perhaps not surprising that Matthew Arnold, writing
from a dreary sojourn at Derby in November 1852, in the early days
of his school inspectorate, told his mother that he had looked long-
ingly in the bright morning to Fledborough, his recollections of it
the only approach he had to the memory of a golden age.

Dr Arnold's family background was in marked contrast. The
Arnolds were of East Anglian stock from the neighbourhood of

Lowestoft, where for generations they had been connected with the sea, owning fish-houses, boats and good yeoman land. Dr Arnold's grandfather and great-uncle both spent their lives in the Excise service; so did his father, William Arnold, Collector of Customs at Cowes, where the famous son was born in 1795. William Arnold married a Delafield, whose brother went to New York, married well, made a fortune and started a family of some distinction there. After the American Revolution John Delafield was made a freeman of New York City; the two families carried on a regular correspondence for a couple of decades.

The Delafields were of Puritan descent and fitted successfully into the American ethos; we remember that Matthew Arnold detested narrow-minded Dissent and did not think much of the American ethos.

William Arnold died suddenly, not old; his widow lived on in the house at Cowes, looking after the children. Of these one was an army chaplain; one daughter married an Irish earl, another the Rev. John Buckland. Thomas was the seventh child and youngest son. He was sent to Winchester to school, 1807–11, and always cherished strong Wykehamist feelings, sending his eldest son, Matt, there at first. At sixteen Thomas Arnold won a scholarship to Corpus Christi College at Oxford, a small and elect society where he made a number of friends who distinguished themselves, among them John Keble and the Devonshireman, who became Judge Coleridge.

Elected Fellow of Oriel Arnold joined the most gifted group going at Oxford at the time. The golden age there had begun with the Noetics – chief among them, the Rev. John Davison – who showed themselves capable of answering the secularizing Edinburgh Reviewers on their own ground. Davison and Whately (subsequently Archbishop) had a distinct influence on Newman, Whately in logic and casuistry. It was said that Oriel Common Room 'stank of logic'. This was not Keble's line of country: he took more agreeably to poetry. At this time he was a close friend of Arnold, and became a precursor of Matthew Arnold as Professor of Poetry.

There was already some doubt about Thomas Arnold's entire orthodoxy as to doctrine, as we learn from a friend's letter to Coleridge: particularly with regard to 'that most awful one, on which all *very* inquisitive reasoning minds are, I believe, most liable to such temptations – I mean the doctrine of the blessed Trinity. Do not start, my dear Coleridge: I do not believe that Arnold has any serious scruples of the *understanding* about it' . . . etc. We see the kind of nonsense they tormented themselves with, quarrelled about and broke friendships over. Arnold and Keble's early friendship broke under this strain.

As we have seen they both stayed at Fledborough with their friend Trevenen Penrose, and there Arnold's fate was settled by meeting Mary in 1819. Arnold had already left Oxford to join his brother-in-law Buckland in running a preparatory school in the village of Laleham by the Thames. There they had two large Georgian houses, of which Buckland's remains. Arnold brought there his widowed mother, his sister and an aunt Delafield; next year, 1820, he added a wife – the place became something of an Arnold colony, subsequently a shrine. Matthew Arnold was born there on Christmas Eve 1822, and there he is buried in the family grave with his wife and three young sons, in the shadow of the red-brick church tower – today the traffic swirling around what was once a quiet Thames-side churchyard.

Arnold was blissfully busy and happy in his family life at Laleham. He was a shy man, but his marriage released him into happiness and relaxed his somewhat formal manner. He was able to carry forward his studies, in 1825 discovering Niebuhr, who revolutionized his conception of Roman history. (If only Newman had been able to read German, someone regretted, what a difference it would have made!) Arnold was beginning to write, his mind broadened by frequent visits to the Continent. Already his sympathies and interests were much wider than those of his Oxford colleagues: he inherited the family interest in ships and the sea, he had a passion for geography and travel. He was a liberal-minded reformer, passionately concerned with the state of the country needing reform; he was beginning to write his hot-headed pamphlets – everything about him was vehement and passionate: so unlike his son.

In 1824 Arnold made the acquaintance of Wordsworth, who became something of a tutelary deity in the family. The old sage, who had been through the French Revolution and knew what revolution meant and how much liberal illusions were worth, had a real respect and affection for his optimistic young friend. It says much for them both, for they constantly disagreed; once, after a tirade from Wordsworth against the way things were going, all that Arnold said was: 'What beautiful English the old man speaks!' Later, when Arnold built the family home there in the Lake District, Fox How, Wordsworth supervised the building operations for him away at Rugby. The cult of Wordsworth and the devotion to the mountains were carried over to the next generation, with Matthew.

If only the family had looked westward to Cornwall! –

But westward, look, the land is bright!

– as Matt's greatest friend at Oxford, Clough, wrote. It was Dr Arnold who directed the family northwards, from Rugby, and made Fox How their pole-star. Only once did he bring his young family down to Cornwall to stay with Admiral Penrose at Ethy, in 1826. And the Fledborough Penroses came to congregate more and more in that neighbourhood. Arnold's friend Trevenen Penrose, who had been born at Crannick, became vicar of Coleby and a prebendary of Lincoln; three unmarried sisters lived with him at Coleby, off the highway from Grantham to Lincoln, six Penrose gravestones in the churchyard there. Grandfather Penrose's eldest son lived most of his life at Bracebridge and died at Langton by Wragby. His eldest son became a master at Rugby; another son was headmaster of Sherborne, but ended up with a living in Lincolnshire; a third son, Francis Cranmer Penrose, was architect and surveyor of St Paul's cathedral, and wrote a good deal about architecture. (Frank Penrose, a fine big fellow, was Kingsley's friend at Cambridge, the original of Amyas Leigh in *Westward Ho!*) His daughter, Dame Emily Penrose, was the chief architect of the success of Somerville College, Oxford, in her time the foremost of the women's colleges. All the Penroses were scribblers of one sort or another; we see how wholly directed they were to the Church and education.

19

Arnold was perfectly happy at Laleham, but the call came to him to take on the difficult headmastership of Rugby. The Public Schools at this time were not only – as I have heard them described by an old Evangelical – 'sinks of iniquity', but tough assignments requiring courage. A riot at Rugby in 1797 was so serious that soldiers had to be called in to quell it; so too at Winchester – a particularly rough school in the nineteenth century – in 1770 and again in 1818. It was Dr Arnold's fate to be associated with both. When he accepted the call to Rugby his aim was specifically to try out whether his ideas of Christian education were practicable. In the famous testimonial the Provost of Oriel wrote for him he said that, if elected, Arnold 'would change the face of education all through the Public Schools of England.' In the fifteen years he had there, 1827–42, he certainly set the process going.

He was an inspired teacher: because he was so ardently concerned with what was going forward in his time, he had a way of making the past live. In his earlier years there he was an exceedingly controversial character – Dean Stanley refers in his official biography, which so much helped to canonize him, to 'the vehement outcry with which he used to be assailed'. We do not need to go into the new methods he introduced – the concentration on Chapel and the religious side of school life, the responsibility he placed on his famous VIth form for the moral tone as well as the discipline of the school; that is not our subject.

He was a reformer who lashed out at abuses in constant pamphlets, articles, regular journalism – and with school trustees, a bench of conservative country gentlemen, who several times thought of dismissing him. The Doctor positively asked for trouble, elicited enemies on several fronts. He was outraged by the Oxford Malignants, as he termed the Tractarians, with their deliberate reversal of the movement towards reform, the return to medievalism, the credulity mingled with the disingenuous subtlety of Newman's mind. Newman retorted sweetly with the poisoned question: 'But is Dr Arnold a Christian?' – he could not but admire the Doctor's very masculine personality, himself a feminine type.

The personality, indeed, was overwhelming – that was the fact about him, and what kept his legend alive among his boys for the rest of the century: they hero-worshipped him. But his great-grandson, Arnold Whitridge, has realized in our time: 'a later generation has been able to infer that things would not have gone so well at Laleham and at Rugby without her [Mrs Arnold's] presence. Stanley, who adored her, pays tribute to her 'judgment, courage, decision'. Not less important was her tact, calming the Doctor down, smoothing down the aggressiveness, the controversial sharpness. She seems to have prevailed on him to abjure controversy in his later years. *Tom Brown's Schooldays*, which broadcast his fame and Rugby's all over the world, was dedicated to her.

It was his effect on the boys that was so remarkable, all the more so because he was not individually interested in boys – he had the gift of summing up their character at a glance. And he had no illusions about their morals – the chief concern of his remarkable, and deadly earnest, sermons in Chapel. It was his favourite pupils who carried his message all over the world – though he elicited an astonishing loyalty among the ordinary run of the mill: eight Cave baronets in succession went to Rugby. The Doctor was keenly interested in the colonies – at one time he thought he would like a colonial bishopric. A favourite pupil, John Gell, went to Tasmania; whither Arnold's younger son Tom followed as Director of Education, after a spell in New Zealand where the alert Doctor had bought 200 acres.

His best classical scholar was C. J. Vaughan, who carried over his influence into Harrow, where he made a gifted Headmaster – though he differed from the Doctor in being so much interested individually in his VIth formers that he had to resign, and was ever afterwards denied preferment. But for this *contretemps* he was expected to become Archbishop of Canterbury – instead of which, a Headmaster of Wellington, Benson, an excessive beater, succeeded to the throne of St Augustine.

None of these was a man of genius; but Arthur Clough, another Celt – whom Mrs Arnold made a member of the family, in the absence of his own in America – had a touch of genius. He became the chief friend of Matt, who had much more.

And what of the Doctor's influence on his eldest son, and the son's reaction to the Doctor? Among all the faithful devotees at Rugby, Matt seems to have stood out as the only one who escaped the impact: besides being very different in type, he was throughout his early life in obvious reaction against his father.

Matt was not strong in early childhood; he wore iron braces on his legs to counteract rickets, and he had a hesitation in his speech – a sure sign of something *psychologisch* in the background. Later he grew strong and athletic, much given to walking and running and swimming; as a young man he was rather handsome, with very different looks from his father's. Nothing of the Doctor's blunt honest features; Matt's long nose came from the Trevenens, his distinguished, melancholy cast of face with the refined, rather supercilious expression certainly did not come from East Anglia, nor the raven-black hair which would not turn grey even when he was quite elderly.

He was not his father's favourite; this was Tom, a better scholar who achieved a Double First at Oxford – but would have disappointed his father much more by his subsequent erratic course, going over to Newman. 'Matt does not know what it is to work', said the Doctor, who hardly knew what it was to do anything else; he found the boy affectionate enough, but he would do no *earnest reading*. Evidently Matt withdrew behind a mask, confronted by the barrage from this dynamo; he continued to wear a mask, in public and often even in private relations, all his life. The Doctor simply could not understand Matt, who defeated him, and then surprised this bluff, straightforward English type.

Tom Arnold, in his *Passages in a Wandering Life*, confesses that 'in a sense, we were *afraid*' of their father, especially if they did anything wrong. He says of Matt at school: 'ratiocination did not at that time charm him; and the demonstration of what he cared to know found him languid.' The later Matthew Arnold, though no boring metaphysician, found no difficulty in reasoning; but evidently he trusted his intuitions, more rewarding for the developing genius within, and fed his mind on what he fancied rather than what was forced upon him with such moral earnestness. The recalcitrance went deeper and was altogether more significant than merely making faces behind the

Doctor's chair, which he was observed to do at Rugby.

He had first been sent to Winchester; his career there ended in a no less significant way. Tom tells us that Matt spoke too freely; one day he said briskly to the Headmaster that he did not have to take trouble, he found the work in his form so light and easy. This piece of superciliousness was overheard by a senior boy; it was reported and made Matt very unpopular – he was pelted with potato peelings in the Great School. He was withdrawn from Winchester, but not before he had won the school prize for reciting poetry – with a bravado speech from Byron's 'Marino Faliero'.

While at Winchester the two boys used to walk over to Hursley, where Keble, who was Matt's godfather, was rector. Matthew Arnold always treated the Oxford Movement with respect; and at Oxford used regularly to attend Newman's sermons in St Mary's, though they had no intellectual influence with him whatever – on both counts in complete contrast with his father. What Matt so much admired in Newman, he said, was his *manner*; that influenced him, but – come to think of it – could anything be more deflating?

At Rugby Matt continued on his own way and followed his own inclinations, so reserved that there is little information about him. But we can look into the youth's inner nature in the prize poem he wrote, 'Alaric at Rome', and recited at Rugby 12 June 1840. It is usual to dismiss this poem as a mere school exercise; this is imperceptive, for it revealingly foreshadows the mature poet, not only in character and thought but even in tricks of speech. The subject came from Gibbon, the motto from Byron; but the poem is not at all Byronic: there is no passion and no clash of action, it is meditative and elegiac. An early stanza announces a theme the mature Arnold would often return to:

> *Yes, there are stories registered on high,*
> *Yes, there are stains time's fingers cannot blot . . .*
> *Yet some there are, their very lives would give*
> *To be remembered thus, and yet they cannot live.*

No grandeur of conquest or pride of a conqueror appears as it would have done in Byron, but the lament:

Where all we see, or do, or hear, or say,
Seems strangely echoed back by tones of yesterday. . . .

Thy dead are kings, thy dust are palaces,
Relics of nations thy memorial stones;
And the dim glories of departed days
Fold like a shroud around thy withered bones;
And o'er thy towers the wind's half-uttered sigh
Whispers, in mournful tones, thy silent elegy.

Nature itself is given an elegiac note:

Has thou not marked on a wild autumn day
When the wind slumbereth in a sudden lull,
What deathlike stillness o'er the landscape lay,
How calmly sad, how sadly beautiful;
How each bright tint of tree, and flower, and heath,
Were mingling with the sere and withered hues of death.

Here is the inner spirit of young Matt Arnold, for all his gay companionship and bravado on the surface, melancholy within, as all through life: no conquering Alaric.

Perchance his wandering heart was far away,
Lost in dim memories of his earlier home . . .
One little year: that restless soul shall rest,
That frame of vigour shall be crumbling clay,
And tranquilly, above that troubled breast,
The sunny waters hold their joyous way.

And, for conclusion:

A little while, alas! a little while,
And the same world has tongue, and ear, and eye,
The careless glance, the cold unmeaning smile,
The thoughtless word, the lack of sympathy!
Who would not turn him from the barren sea
And rest his weary eyes on the green land and thee!

Here, at the end, is recognizable vintage Arnold at seventeen and a half!

That same year the youth who took things so easily won the Balliol scholarship. The Doctor was astonished.

CHAPTER 2

Oxford

THE OXFORD WHICH young Arnold came up to in 1841 was in the full tide of Newman's Movement. It was the liveliest and most intriguing thing going in the university, but it was very much a minority movement, its mission directed to the Church rather than the university. Most colleagues remained unaffected by it – the 'aristocratic whist-club of All Souls' for one – and it was undergraduates and clerics who crowded St Mary's to fall for the subtle charm of Newman's preaching.

Dr Arnold's eldest son was a frequent attendant; Tom, who came up with a scholarship to University College in 1842, eventually succumbed to the casuistical seducer. It is all the more remarkable that, as Tom wrote, Newman's '*teaching* never made an impression' upon his brother. Matthew recorded later that he liked Newman's 'general disposition of mind rather than a particular set of ideas'. This was pretty superior – and discerning – in so young a man; at the scholars' table at Balliol he would argue that 'the strict imposition of creeds had done more to break up than to unite churches, and nations, and families.'

It was a very individual young man who could thus hold aloof in an atmosphere of acute partisanship, a tribute to his inner maturity of mind. His lifelong friend, John Duke Coleridge – to become Lord Chief Justice – son of Dr Arnold's old friend, became a Tractarian: 'Credo in Newmannum.'[1] All his life Matthew held his father's opponent in high esteem, and went out of his way to express it, but

---

[1] Oddly enough, J. D. Coleridge had been at Helston Grammar School in Cornwall with Charles Kingsley.

it was the style, the urbanity, that he admired. Newman asserted that he had never attacked the Doctor; he must have forgotten – as people do – the barbed question: 'But is Dr Arnold a Christian?'

Matthew found throughout life that all doors were opened to him as the son of his famous father: it was a great advantage. The point is made by his Balliol friend, Shairp, who later succeeded him as Professor of Poetry, and described him as he appeared at this time:

> *The one wide-welcomed for a father's fame,*
> *Entered with free bold step that seemed to claim*
> *Fame for himself, not on another lean.*
>
> *So full of power, yet blithe and debonair,*
> *Rallying his friends with pleasant banter gay,*
> *Or half-adream chanting with jaunty air*
> *Great words of Goethe, catch of Béranger,*
> *We see the banter sparkle in his prose,*
> *But knew not then the undertone that flows*
> *So calmly sad, through all his stately lay.*

There was the enigma: the undercurrent of melancholy (from which actually the poetry came) beneath a gay surface, full of banter and persiflage, high good humour and teasing spirits. I suspect that all this was a defence mechanism, conscious or unconscious, with which he protected his abnormally sensitive inner self.

Another crux in his make-up is seized on by his friend: Arnold's *latent* power – for at Balliol he exerted himself no more than he had done at Rugby. He neglected his reading of the classical text-books; he never became a good pure scholar, unlike his brother Tom – or, for that matter, the Doctor himself. Matthew fed on what he fancied, Goethe and Wordsworth, contemporary French poetry – the best way for a man of budding genius. All his life he was devoted to French literature, and he much over-estimated German. It is difficult to appreciate his passion for George Sand, to which he remained loyal to the end, until we realize what a liberating influence she was from the intense moralizing he had been subjected to. (*That* influence from the Doctor, alas, remained with him.)

In this year, 1841, the Doctor was appointed Regius Professor of

Modern History and returned to Oxford to a triumphant reception in December for his Inaugural Lecture. He loved his old university: 'it always grieves me to hear that a man does not like Oxford. I was so happy there myself, and above all so happy in my friends.' All the Arnolds shared this feeling: his son was to write the most enduring tributes to the scene in literature.

The reception was something of a demonstration: all the family and Rugby disciples were present. The university turned up to greet the controversial figure, on his return after years, in such numbers that the Lecture had to be moved to the Sheldonian Theatre. At forty-six the Doctor was at the peak of his reputation, poised for a new career: he would do for English history what Guizot had done for French history with his lectures at the Collège de France. (No one would say of Dr Arnold what a French wit said of Guizot: *il avait l'air de savoir de toute éternité ce qu'il a appris le matin.*)

The following summer, with all the promise of the ideas for the future he had seething within him, Dr Arnold was suddenly struck down. His unexpected death was a veritable shock to the country, registered so far afield as India and Tasmania: the sudden extinction of such a dynamo left a great void, even apart from the Victorian cult of death. Tom, as he stood by his father's body, was stunned; Matthew's reaction was a cooler one, the curious reflection as the family gathered round that 'their sole source of *information* was gone, that all they had ever known was contained in that lifeless head'. It was years before he paid his tribute to him in 'Rugby Chapel', and even then only in reply to an attack upon his father's memory:

> *Fifteen years have gone round*
> *Since thou arosest to tread,*
> *In the summer morning, the road*
> *Of death, at a call unforeseen,*
> *Sudden. For fifteen years,*
> *We who till then in thy shade*
> *Rested as under the boughs*
> *Of a mighty oak, have endured*
> *Sunshine and rain as we might,*

Bare, unshaded, alone,
Lacking the shelter of thee.

A perceptive poetic ear can tell that this is a *willed* poem, not an inspired one like 'The Scholar Gipsy'.

The family closed ranks around that overwhelming memory. Mrs Arnold moved into the position of its leader, a largish family not one of whom was yet through university or out in the world. She was well qualified to fill it: Archbishop Whately recognized her clear intelligence and her wisdom. It is remarkable to observe, in the immense correspondence she kept up for many years, with what intuitive sense and tact she directed a family of individuals, most of them distinguished in various ways, marked by the divergent strains within them. It was she who imposed upon them the cult of Dr Arnold, as religiously as Queen Victoria did that of the Prince Consort. She remained for decades beside the lamp in the family shrine at Fox How, to which all the family looked and were ever returning; she inculcated the devotion to the father which came in the end to influence their eldest son.

After Dr Arnold's death it was he, not Newman, who prevailed at Oxford with the liberal generation that went ahead with reform, after the fever aroused by Newman had spent itself.

Meanwhile, Matt was at Balliol, not getting on with his work. He was more often out of doors, sometimes with the Harriers and hounds, hunting. He was popular now for his cheerful, bantering ways, and he was not one to impose himself on anybody. New buildings were already taking the place at Balliol of the old Rats' Castle, where Southey had conceived his nonsense about pantisocracy. Not that Matt didn't dream dreams – his sympathies were liberal, all for the well-being of the people; but his projects were mainly poetic, and he kept them to himself. Max Müller remembered him, with German sentimentalism, 'as a young man beautiful, strong and manly, full of dreams and schemes. His Olympian manners began even at Oxford. . . . The sound of his voice and the wave of his arm were Jove-like.'

Breakfasts and wines were the fashion. He and his friends formed a society, the Decade, nearly all of them to achieve reputation and make their contribution to the life of a country then worth making a contribution to – at the peak of its power and prosperity, the first in the world. In itself this was an incentive to achieve something. There were Jowett, Temple, Shairp, Lake, Stanley, Clough – all men of promise who fulfilled their promise in various ways and left their mark.

But what was Matt going to do? He certainly did not exemplify the Doctor's moral earnestness. He was a poseur and a dandy, given to sport and banter, and even playing pranks; he would not be 'wholly serious', as Max Beerbohm portrayed the humourless Mrs Humphry Ward beseeching her Uncle Matt to be. Stanley, on his way to the Deanery of Westminster, deplored the 'qualities which gave much alarm to many'. J. D. Coleridge, on a coach journey with Matt, was amused and irritated by the coolness with which he took advantage of the credulity of the passengers to persuade them that Coleridge was 'a poor mad gent whose keeper he was'. His friends condoled with each other: 'Matt utters as many absurdities as ever, with as grave a face, and I am afraid wastes his time considerably. . . . But advice does not go for much with him.'

Most of all was the serious-minded Clough concerned. Of all the Rugby pupils he was closest to the Doctor, and took most of his moral imprint; prematurely and priggishly, he worried himself over the morals of his fellows, taking the Headmaster's burdens upon his youthful shoulders. Original and gifted, a sensitive Celt, he was the inspiration of the *Rugby Magazine*, celebrated in its day. He had won the Balliol scholarship four years before Matt, and went on to join the most distinguished group in Oxford as a Fellow of Oriel.

What golden times they had, when all the world was young; life lay before them, their sympathies – led by Clough – were all for the people and the liberal hopes that were to lead to the revolutions of 1848 over Europe. They were sympathetic to the Chartists, which Dr Arnold was far from being: he pointed out angrily that liberal causes were a very different thing from popular causes. (History has shown that the Doctor was right.) His two sons, and his pupils,

Clough and Theo Walrond, formed an inner circle. They breakfasted together every Sunday in Clough's rooms and discussed the portents and signs of the world around them: Peel's reforms, Carlyle and Chartism, Emerson and his Transcendentalism, Wordsworth and the new poetry of Tennyson, and – rather shocking – George Sand. For the rest they went skiffing up the Cherwell, down the Thames to Iffley and Sandford, upriver to Bablockhythe; or wandered round the hills to Cumnor, Hinksey which then had its haunted mansion, the sign with Sibylla's name, the signal elm at Fyfield which was a symbol for them.

But young Matt would not work. Clough went up to Fox How as a pacemaker one vacation, and found Mrs Arnold rather anxious about him. Clough reported: 'should I relax in the least my yoke-fellow would at once come to a dead stop.' Even with Schools approaching he could not be got up to four hours' work a day. Clough thought a Second above his deserts, 'but I do not think he can drop below it, and one would not be surprised if he rose above it in spite of all his ignorance.' In the event he got a Second, which was the same as Clough had done for all his application. With this disappointing result he took refuge for a few months at Rugby, teaching the Lower Vth – and then surprised people again by winning the first Fellowship at Oriel, just thirty years after his father's election. Mrs Arnold was 'well pleased, as also is the Venerable Poet at Rydal, who had taken Matt under his special protection as a Second classman. I hope it will do Matt no harm, and he is certainly improved since the disaster of November.'

In the intimacy of Oriel Common Room as Fellows together, Matt was to find in Clough his chief friend, who mattered most to him intellectually. Clough was a man of original bent of mind, and keen, wide-ranging interests, for ever seeking and searching, without finding satisfaction or a resting place. The difference of an undergraduate generation, a mere four years, means much at the university. Clough had the advantage of being Arnold's senior; Matt had the advantage of being inwardly more mature and a better poet to be. This led to a certain awkwardness in their relations.

There was another difficulty. For all Matt's gaiety and banter, addressing Clough as 'My love', 'My dearest', 'My dear love', Arnold's was a cooler nature. (All the Arnolds were heterosexual to a fault.) Others of his men friends complained of his coolness: Coleridge for one reproached him 'with a want of interest' in his friends. Matt had to defend himself: 'I laugh too much and they make one's laughter mean too much.' They thought that he was laughing at them – as perhaps he was – and when he was serious, they couldn't tell. Coleridge had little sense of humour: he became a great Victorian, made a fortune at the bar, ended as Lord Chief Justice, and built a fearsome house at Ottery St Mary, where Matt stayed with him in later years.

Staying with him earlier, Arnold fell for the beauty of the West Country – if only he had explored further, where so many of his roots were, the soil whence so much of his nature came! When his father's Sermons came out, he recommended them to Coleridge as 'the most delightful and the most satisfactory to read of all his writings'. Evidently Matt did not care for the impulsiveness and vehemence of the pamphleteering. To recommend them to Coleridge, a High Churchman, Matt tactfully saw no reason in the Sermons to change his admiration for Newman: 'owing to my utter want of prejudice I find it perfectly possible to admire them both.'

Though the friendship with Coleridge lasted all their lives, that with Clough, who died early, was much more important to the growing poet.

It was poetry that chiefly occupied his inner mind during those years, which came to fruition with his first volume, *A Strayed Reveller*, in 1849, while Clough was occupied with his 'Ambarvalia'. What else occupied Matt is extraordinarily difficult to find out, for by his own instructions his correspondence at Fox How was destroyed – up to 1848. We have only his poems to go on, most of those undated, and we have to read back from later references in his own work. What was there to conceal?

In 1843 he had won the Newdigate with his poem on Cromwell – a subject much in the air through Carlyle. The heroic figure did not inspire him, and Arnold himself thought the poem less good than his schoolboy effort on Alaric, as it is. Oddly enough, the best lines are those describing Laud, who evidently appealed to him more. Arnold never reprinted either poem. But his sonnet on Shakespeare, written next year, 1844, was reprinted many times during his life, is very famous because of the subject, has been innumerably anthologized, and done a great deal of damage. For it rests on a fundamental misconception of Shakespeare.

We should not take it too seriously, for it is a young man's view, written at twenty-two, and Arnold knew nothing whatever of Shakespeare's age, time or circumstances.

> *And thou, who didst the stars and sunbeams know,*
> *Self-schooled, self-scanned, self-honoured, self-secure,*
> *Didst walk on Earth unguessed at. Better so!*

This is youthful ignorance: Shakespeare was recognized the most popular and successful dramatist of his time, and even we know more about him than any other of his contemporary dramatists. And so the too famous lines –

> *Others abide our question. Thou art free.*
> *We ask and ask: Thou smilest and art still,*
> *Out-topping knowledge . . .*

– are largely nonsense. The constant quotation of this youthful effort, sanctioned by Arnold's subsequent authority, has had the obscurantist effect of discouraging inquiry. It is obscurantist to say that Shakespeare out-tops knowledge, and to suggest that while others abide our question, he is beyond it. This is what is meant by bardolatry; the real scholar knows that Shakespeare is to be understood and appreciated along with other writers of his time, Spenser, Sidney, Donne, but especially alongside his fellow-dramatists, Marlowe and Ben Jonson.

However, we should not take seriously this pompous pronouncement at twenty-two, for all that it has had such a deleterious effect on criticism.

Arnold's three sonnets devoted to the great French actress, Rachel, are far finer; they were written much later, but they betray what he was doing in 1846–47. He was a good deal in Paris. He first saw her act in London in the summer of 1846; from late December to mid-February he was in Paris, where he went to the theatre practically every night, often to see her. His enthusiasm for George Sand led him to make a pilgrimage to Nohant to pay his respects – but he imparted the information in the security of thirty years later when she was safely dead.

'It seems to me but the other day that I saw her, yet it was in the August of 1846, more than thirty years ago. I saw her in her own Berry, at Nohant, where she returned to live after she became famous, where she died and now has her grave.' He goes on, a little disingenuously, to a magical evocation of the countryside that had so charmed him in her books, as if it were only the landscape that called him to her. He had written her a letter, expressing his homage; the promiscuous, hardly satiable lady replied with an invitation to the young man to visit her.

'The midday breakfast was not yet over when I reached the house, and I found a large party assembled. I entered with some trepidation, as well I might . . . but the simplicity of Madame Sand's manner put me at ease in a moment.' She introduced him to the others, including Chopin 'with his wonderful eyes' – he was not yet entirely overlaid. 'Madame Sand made me sit by her'; they touched on many themes, including Switzerland whither Arnold was bound. 'After breakfast she led the way into the garden, gathered a flower or two and gave them to me, shook hands heartily at the gate, and I saw her no more.'

We know the impression the handsome Englishman had on the impressionable Madame Sand: she described it as *l'effet d'un Milton jeune et voyageant*. We should remember that to her Milton was a memorable Puritan. The young man went safe on his way to Switzerland. In a later year, he played with the idea of a return journey to Nohant, but thought better of it.

Later that century Henry James also paid his pilgrimage to Nohant, when the siren was dead. Looking up at the bedroom windows he said, 'Which of those rooms did she sleep in, I wonder?'; then, with a pause, 'but – ah! – which of those rooms did she not sleep in?'

Rumours of Arnold's rampaging about the Continent passed

round among his friends. Clough: 'Matt is just come back from Paris; his stay at the latter end seems to have been very satisfactory to him. . . .' A little later: 'Matt is full of Parisianism; theatres in general, and Rachel in special: he enters the room with a chanson of Béranger's on his lips – for the sake of the French words almost conscious of tune [he had no ear for music: a masculine trait]. His carriage shows him in fancy parading the Rue de Rivoli – and his hair is guiltless of English scissors. He breakfasts at twelve, and never dines in Hall, and in the week or eight days rather (for a Sunday must be included) he has been to Chapel *once*. . . .' A fortnight later, to Shairp: 'what evil report hath come to your ears concerning Matt? Wherefore Snub?'

What else had he been up to in Paris? We know only that during those six weeks he unwontedly spent a great deal of money, on theatres, fares, clothes, books and entertaining others. He was having his fling.

At Fox How, at the shrine, Mrs Arnold was becoming concerned again, and 'very anxious he should have something regular in the way of employment'. So it was his mother's influence that persuaded him to take the decisive step of leaving Oxford and taking a job, as secretary to Lord Lansdowne, President of the Council, the minister primarily responsible for education. Clough continues: 'quite a mistake, I think, on her part; but Matt does not seem to dislike the prospect, though he has no intention of making this his permanent line.'

On the contrary, Mrs Arnold, as usual, was right in her judgment: it was the step that led on to Matthew Arnold's lifelong career in education. When he went back to Oxford, on his temporary visits as Professor of Poetry over ten years, he returned with achievement to his credit and acclaim: like his father.

CHAPTER 3

Marguerite

THE YEARS 1848–51 were as crucial and decisive in Arnold's life as those of 1592–94 were in Shakespeare's. Unexpectedly we know more now, definitely and definitively, what was happening to the Elizabethan Shakespeare at the core of his being than to the Victorian Arnold. But Shakespeare's nature was open and free, as his friends testified; Arnold's was reserved and controlled, and besides this he took extraordinary steps to cover his tracks, apart from the evidences he left in the poems about Marguerite in Switzerland, which he himself said were those that came closest to his heart. We know now who Shakespeare's dark lady was – it was always obvious who the young lord of the Sonnets and the rival poet for his patronage were; but we shall never know who Arnold's Marguerite was, though she made an undying impression upon the poet and left so many traces in his poetry.

Externally his career is clear, and conventional, enough. The worldling in him – how unlike the Doctor! – took with avidity to the grand social and political life at Lansdowne House, the splendid mansion at the bottom of Berkeley Square. It has now vanished, but we may conjure up something of the highest Whig society, refined and intellectual, that gathered round that hospitable table from the exquisite Adam dining-room that remains, preserved in pickle, in the Metropolitan Museum in New York. The young bachelor had lodgings in Mayfair, at 101 Mount Street, and shuttled to and fro between Lansdowne House and the Marquis's vast country seat, Bowood in Wiltshire.

At New Year 1848 we find him writing to his mother on his way to Bowood: he had taken the opportunity to call in on his aunt at

Laleham and see the former family servants and folks who remembered him. 'I was yesterday at the old house and under the cedars
and by the old pink acacia. . . . The paved part of the barge-road on
the Laleham side of the lock-house is all as it was, and the campanulas,
they told me, grow as much as ever there in summer.' He always
remained addicted to Thames-side and bathing in the river; shortly
we hear of him taking a header into it by the kempshott (i.e. landing-
stage), with Tom Hughes of *Tom Brown's Schooldays* and Chartist
sympathies.

In London, besides his closeness to the highest political society,
often crossing the Park to attend a debate in Parliament, he had a
front-seat view of the culminating Chartist events and the mob in
Trafalgar Square that spring. He thought that 'the hour of hereditary
peerage and eldest sonship and immense properties has, I am convinced, as Lamartine would say, struck.' This was a young man's
view, like the absurdity of his view of Shakespeare: those things are
still with us, more than a century after.

So too with the France of 1848, regarding France as '*politically* in
the van of Europe; it is the *intelligence* of their *idea-moved masses*
which makes them, politically, as far superior to the *insensible masses*
of England as to the Russian serfs.' The hopes of the rather bloody
Revolution of 1848 were shortly succeeded by the liberal fatuity of
the Second Republic, closed down upon by the *coup d'état* of 1851
and the autocracy of the Second Empire. The masses were what they
always had been, much the same everywhere, as Shakespeare knew
them to be. Arnold's views were those of a young man on such
matters, not to be taken seriously. He shortly recovered his equi-
librium politically, as Clough, an immature soul, never did. Clough
regarded Arnold's recovery as a return to 'cynicism'; this it was not:
Arnold was never a cynic, he had a well-justified pessimism about
human nature. The muddled are apt to confuse pessimism with
cynicism.

In March Arnold was present at the riots in Trafalgar Square; in
April he attended the Chartist Convention and 'was much struck
with the ability of the speakers'. Spouting, however, was the only
thing such people as Feargus O'Connor were any good at: when it

came to action, the Chartist threat melted like snows in spring, the great London demonstration dispersed by the violence of a downpour of rain. By July Clough reports, 'Matt was at one time really heated to a very fervid enthusiasm, but he has become sadly cynical again of late. However, I think the poetism goes on favourably.' Arnold was one of those who learned from experience; in such times poetry was an inner refuge to resort to, at all times more rewarding than the ephemera of politics. He was writing verse all through the 1840s, to come before the public with his first volume next year, in 1849.

Life at Lansdowne House had its poetic side; he had time on his hands for reading and writing. To his favourite sister 'K', he describes a magical moment in the great house one evening in May 1848: 'it is beginning to grow dusk, but it has been a sweet day, with sun and a playing wind and a softly broken sky. The crocuses, which have long starred the lawn in front of the windows, growing like daisies out of the turf, have nearly vanished; but the lilacs that border the court are thrusting their leaves out to make amends.' There follow some lines of poetry; then, 'it grows more and more gray and indistinct, and the musical clock behind me is quickening its pace in preparation for its half-hour peal.' So powerful is his evocation, one is in the room with him there.

When Charlotte Brontë met him about this time she was put off by his seeming 'foppery'; little did she suspect how much the young dandy disapproved of her *Villette* for its lack of reserve and self-control. Mrs Arnold, when she came up to town for a glimpse of her son against his glittering background, had a more modest reaction: the widow of the Doctor, more used to scholastic and clerical society, could not but be proud of her son but felt out of place among all the notabilities he frequented. Unknown to them all, Matt was undergoing an inner development which was a surprise to them when revealed in his first volume of poems.

To this development the major emotional experience of his life, which took place in the freer atmosphere of Switzerland, largely contributed; its evidences, and its lasting effects, in memory and inspiration, are observable in later volumes and over many years.

In September 1848 Arnold went to Switzerland in pursuit of Obermann, as nostalgic writers do, for Obermann (i.e. Senancour) had
much influenced him.[1] There, in the way nature has of imitating art,
Arnold met with an experience much like Obermann's – or, perhaps,
he was already disposed to receive it. Like many another young
Englishman of the upper middle class he found abroad a liberating
experience from the close embrace of convention, family, the Doctor
and all that. It was in the fashionable Hotel Bellevue at Thun that
he encountered the grey-blue eyes that turned his head and might
have settled his fate, but did not quite – though their memory and
the memory of her thrilling voice remained with him always.

We know that her name was Marguerite and very little else, for
he destroyed all evidence outside the poems that express his emotions.
Some have surmised that the girl belonged to the lower classes and
may even have been a servant; inherently improbable, this is put out
of question by his poem on returning the Letters of Ortis she had lent
him – a taste for reading Ugo Foscolo would hardly have been
shared by a servant-girl.

Where the Sonnets of Shakespeare are in perfectly intelligible
order, there is no such chronological order in Arnold's Marguerite
poems; in later editions he not only altered the order and changed
titles and words but divided them up, placing other poems between
them to break up sequence and put people off the mark. In quoting
them I shall retain the original titles and words as more revealing. 'To
my Friends who Ridiculed a Tender Leave-taking' was reprinted as
'A Memory Picture'; the refrain,

> *Ere the parting kiss be dry,*
> *Quick, thy tablets, Memory!*

became

> *Ere the parting hour go by*
> *Quick, thy tablets, Memory!*

---

[1] Arnold had no ear for music, and so is hardly likely to have known Liszt's
comparable response and magical evocation in his 'Vallée d'Obermann', in *Les
Années de Pélerinage*.

This poem, written after his first visit, describes her for us:

Paint that lilac kerchief, bound
Her soft face, her hair around:
Tied under the archest chin
Mockery ever ambushed in.
Let the fluttering fingers streak
All her pale, sweet-rounded cheek.

Paint that figure's pliant grace
As she towards me leaned her face,
Half refused and half resigned,
Murmuring, 'Art thou still unkind?'

What does this mean – that he held back? So it would seem from a poem of next year, his return visit.

Many a broken promise then
Was new made – to break again.

Marguerite says: 'As last you went,
So the coming year'll be spent:
Some day next year, I shall be,
Entering heedless, kissed by thee'.
Ah! I hope – yet, once away,
What may chain us, who can say?

This, natural enough in the circumstances, was a pretty good forecast of what would come about. Meanwhile –

What, my Friends, these feeble lines
Show, you say, my love declines?

Another poem, 'The Voice', tells us more: its lute-like tones

Blew such a thrilling summons to my will
   Yet could not shake it:
Drained all the life my full heart had to spill;
   Yet could not break it.

This was the situation between the two when he left Thun; they evidently kept some contact during the year that elapsed, for she was expecting his return in the following September. These two poems belong to the first visit, for they were in time to be included in the volume of next year, *A Strayed Reveller, and other Poems*, 'By A. 1849'.

After his spell of walking and climbing in the Alps, Arnold had returned to Thun, 'to linger one day at the Hotel Bellevue for the sake of the blue eyes of one of its inmates', thence down the Rhine homewards. Writing to Clough as 'my love' and 'my duck' as usual, he says jauntily that experience with 'women (I hate the word)' was something to be undergone and known: 'we know beforehand all they can teach us: yet we are obliged to learn it directly from them.' There follow some revealing lines, which he never published:

Say this of her:
The day was, Thou wert not: the day will be,
Thou wilt be most unlovely: shall I choose
Thy little moment life of loveliness
Betwixt blank nothing and abhorred decay
To glue my fruitless gaze on, and to pine,
Sooner than those twin reaches of great ime,
When thou art either nought, and so not loved,
Or somewhat, but that most unloveable,
That preface and post-scribe thee? –

This is an unpromising frame of mind for a successful lover – to be so reflective in the midst of the experience: unlikely to transport or carry off its object.

Meanwhile at home, the political excitements of 1848 over, Arnold's mind was occupied with poetry: he was preparing his book. It is in his letters to Clough that he speaks his mind most naturally, intimately and impressively on the subject – really more so than in his professional criticism, apt to be too self-conscious and deliberate. In the letters he speaks unrestrainedly, for himself. My aim is not literary criticism as such, but what throws light on Arnold; and here his relations with Clough are the most revealing.

At the end of 1848 Clough had published his absurdly named *The Bothie of Tobernavuolich*, in rather absurd hexameters. A kind of novel in verse, priding itself on its modernity, not to say modernism, it was being raved about by the younger clique at Oxford. This put Arnold off, 'the age, the poem, even you'. He hardly knew what to say about the poem itself, and for the moment fobbed Clough off with 'more English than European, I said finally, more American than English [Clough was much associated with America, which Arnold had not much opinion of]; and took up Obermann, and refuged myself with him in his forest against your *Zeitgeist*.' Here we see one of the strongest reasons for Arnold's turning to the classics and classical standards in poetry: his early disillusionment with the present, his distaste for modernity. These two closest of friends could hardly be more apart in spirit.

In his next letter Arnold deplores the influence of Keats, in particular upon Tennyson, whom earlier he had admired. What Arnold disliked was a 'confused multitudinousness', the enriched detail, in short, Keats's declared aim of loading every rift with ore. Arnold reacted, more than was good for his own poetry, into plainness of statement, a rather bare clear style. (He had a passion for clear water.) In his next he comes clean about Clough: 'if I were to say the real truth as to your poems in general, as they impress me – it would be this – that they are not *natural*.' He goes on to quote a line of his own, ' "Not deep the Poet sees, but wide" – think of this as you gaze from the Cumnor Hill towards Cirencester and Cheltenham.' Clough was for ever pulling up his roots to see how the roots were getting on, a far too self-conscious process for the creation of real poetry; Arnold's reference to Cumnor and the prospect thence was to have its final expression in 'Thyrsis' when Clough was dead.

Arnold thought the age itself was inimical to poetry (what would he think today?): 'reflect too, as I cannot but do here more and more [in London], how deeply *unpoetical* the age and all one's surroundings are. Not unprofound, not ungrand, not unmoving – but *unpoetical*.' We may comment that the best poet of them all, Tennyson, did not find it so; but he had the wisdom to lead a withdrawn life, and to follow his intuitions and his inspiration, undeflected by doctrine. On the other hand, as a poet he was a victim too of the Victorian Age.

On 23 September 1849 Arnold wrote one of his most telling letters to Clough, while on his second visit to Marguerite at Thun – though all that he says about that is: 'I am here in a curious and not altogether comfortable state: however, tomorrow I carry my aching head to the mountains and to my cousin, the Blümlis Alp.' And he writes out a stanza which was to occur in his poem, 'Parting'. 'In three or four days I shall be back here, and then I must try how soon I can ferociously turn towards England.' He describes the state of mind in which he would be returning: 'my dearest Clough, these are damned times – everything is against one – the height to which knowledge is come, the spread of luxury, our physical enervation, the absence of great *natures*, the unavoidable contact with millions of small ones, newspapers, cities, light profligate friends . . . our own selves, and the sickening consciousness of our difficulties.' He promised himself that when he got back, he would try to avoid newspapers and the talk of the day, frittering away time and energy of mind: 'public opinion consists in a multitude of such excitements.'

Of course, he was right; but his circumstances were such that he could not adhere to such a line of abstention and withdrawal. Tennyson could and did; Browning, fortunately for him, could live in Italy; the Pre-Raphaelites and Swinburne had their own forms of inner alienation and withdrawal. Arnold became a public man, a very great public servant, and the poetry was sacrificed to it.

His first volume had appeared when he was the mature age of twenty-six. It made little impression; few copies were sold, and Arnold withdrew the book from circulation. We need not bother with reviews, unless the reviewer was otherwise a person of interest. Kingsley wrote a querulous and patronizing notice – but Arnold did not think much of him: he thought Kingsley's sensibilities too coarse for poetry. The only review of any value was by a Pre-Raphaelite, W. M. Rossetti, and even he took exception to the haunting refrain of 'The Forsaken Merman' – such asses reviewers are apt to be. The poem became one of the favourite poems of the century; and rightly, for it was an inspired poem, where many of the others, however competent and admired, are deliberate and willed.

The crisis of the affair with Marguerite, at Thun in the autumn of 1849, led to some of his most moving poems; the intensity of the experience, its unhappy ending, corroborating the melancholy and despair at the core of his inner nature, led to yet more poems of beauty, up to 'The Terrace at Berne' even ten years later.

There was the well-remembered scene, with Marguerite waiting for him:

> *Again I see my bliss at hand;*
> *The town, the lake are here.*
> *My Marguerite smiles upon the strand*
> *Unaltered with the year.*

> *I know that graceful figure fair,*
> *That cheek of languid hue;*
> *I know that soft enkerchiefed hair,*
> *And those sweet eyes of blue.*

> *Again I spring to make my choice;*
> *Again in tones of ire*
> *I hear a God's tremendous voice –*
> *'Be counselled, and retire!'*

The admonition of conscience was plain enough: Marguerite was not a suitable choice. The last stanza has the unconscious betrayal of the word 'ambitious': Arnold was ambitious, and Marguerite conflicted with that. So they occupied themselves as before, without coming to the point:

> *Still glides the stream, slow drops the boat*
> *Under the rustling poplars' shade;*
> *Silent the swans beside us float:*
> *None speaks, none heeds – ah, turn thy head.*

> *Let those arch eyes now softly shine,*
> *That mocking mouth grow sweetly bland:*
> *Ah, let them rest, those eyes, on mine;*
> *On mine let rest that lovely hand.*

Marguerite, we know, was French: well might a French girl, however languid, pout a mocking mouth at a handsome young Englishman whose passion was under such control:

> *My pent-up tears oppress my brain,*
> *My heart is swollen with love unsaid:*
> *Ah, let me weep, and tell my pain,*
> *And on thy shoulder rest my head.*

A rather undignified, as well as unsatisfactory, situation when all is said.

A poem called 'Excuse' follows:

> *I too have suffered: yet I know*
> *She is not cold, though she seems so:*
> *She is not cold, she is not light;*
> *But our ignoble souls lack might.*
>
> *She smiles and smiles, and will not sigh,*
> *While we for hopeless passion die;*
> *Yet she could love those eyes declare,*
> *Were but men nobler than they are.*

That means, if the Englishman had the courage to take the risk; in his acute dilemma, he could not. The Frenchwoman's eyes were 'arch'; we may not be wrong in thinking that one side of her would be amused at his hanging back – and a sense of humour is fatal to passion. Or perhaps she wanted marriage, which he could not offer, rather than sexual satisfaction: her 'ears to one demand alone are coy'. Then,

> *It was not love alone that heaved thy breast,*
> *Fair child, it was the bliss within.*
> *Adieu! and say that one, at least,*
> *Was just to what he did not win.*

That is, she had her own spring of happiness within her – part of what had so much drawn him, probably older than she was.

During his year of absence he had remained true:

We were apart; yet, day by day,
I bade my heart more constant be.
I bade it keep the world away,
And grow a home for only thee;
Nor feared but thy love likewise grew,
Like mine, each day, more tried more true.

He describes his return:

My horse's feet beside the lake,
Where sweet the unbroken moonbeams lay,
Sent echoes through the night to wake
Each glistening strand, each heath-fringed bay.

There was the covered bridge familiar to those parts:

The poplar avenue was passed,
And the roofed bridge that spans the stream;
Up the steep street I hurried fast,
Lli by thy taper's starlike beam.

I came! I saw thee rise! – the blood
Poured flushing to thy languid cheek.
Locked in each other's arms we stood,
In tears, with hearts too full to speak.

We note that Arnold uses the word 'languid' of her more than once, and again notes her pale face: it is not beyond the bounds of possibility that Marguerite was in Switzerland, invalidish, for the benefit of her health. And he found, as the days went by, her ardour, her interest in him cool:

Days flew: ah, soon I could discern
A trouble in thine altered air.
Thy hand lay languidly in mine,
Thy cheek was grave, thy speech grew rare.

Though tortured by the dilemma in which he was caught, both within himself and with external circumstances, Arnold remained in love with her; she was not, now, in love with him.

45

> *The fault was grave! I might have known,*
> *What far too soon, alas, I learned –*
> *The heart can bind itself alone,*
> *And faith may oft be unreturned.*
> *Self-swayed our feelings ebb and swell –*
> *Thou lov'st no more: Farewell! Farewell!*

It was in this mood and in these circumstances – head and heart aching, as he told Clough – that he turned his face to the mountains for consolation, as Obermann had done in similar circumstances; and here is something of what lies behind the Obermann poems.

> *Vain is the effort to forget.*
> *Some day I shall be cold, I know,*
> *As is the eternal moonlit snow*
> *Of the high Alps, to which I go –*
> *But ah, not yet, not yet . . .*

Earlier, he had welcomed the thought of the 'storms of love', was ready for the experience, his first; but now –

> *I struggle towards the light – but oh,*
> *While yet the night is chill,*
> *Upon time's barren, stormy flow,*
> *Stay with me, Marguerite, still!*

Her memory stayed with him always, inspiring yet more poems directly, while the experience entered indirectly, yet recognizably, into others that he wrote. When he returned to England, he wrote the fine poem, 'Parting', with the evocation of how she appeared to him:

> *But who is this, by the half-opened door,*
> *Whose figure casts a shadow on the floor?*
> *The sweet blue eyes – the soft, ash-coloured hair –*
> *The cheeks that still their gentle paleness wear –*
> *The lovely lips, with their arch smile, that tells*
> *The unconquered joy in which her spirit dwells –*
> > *Ah! they bend nearer –*
> > *Sweet lips, this way!*

Though we shall never know her name, she is very recognizable; and he tells us something about her past:

> *In the void air towards thee*
> *My strained arms are cast.*
> *But a sea rolls between us –*
> *Our different past.*
>
> *To the lips, ah! of others,*
> *Those lips have been pressed,*
> *And others, ere I was,*
> *Were clasped to that breast.*
>
> *Far, far from each other*
> *Our spirits have grown.*
> *And what heart knows another?*
> *Ah! who knows his own?*

Arnold had known his own heart, his whole being had been upheaved by this experience; but we see that the breach was inevitable, there could not have been a satisfactory resolution of the affair. That did not make it any the less desolating; yet it was precisely that – so strange is the way of fate with poets – that inspired continuing poetry. If the experience had been altogether satisfactory, the affair consummated, there would have been the less inspiration. Now the poet could call upon remembered emotion:

> *Come to me in my dreams, and then*
> *By day I shall be well again.*
> *For then the night will more than pay*
> *The hopeless longing of the day.*

How much he owed to this experience! – as poets do, to experiences that shake them to the depths and shake poetry out of them, however much the suffering they bring with them – as Shakespeare's infatuation for his dark lady brought him. One can always tell with a poet when an authentic inspiration moves him: it reveals itself in the rhythm, the tremor of the lines. This shattering experience, that riveted the mountains of Switzerland upon him,

47

brought him to maturity, taught him the lessons of life that he – hitherto sheltered in the bosom of his family, then too in the family that was Oxford – needed to learn. These appear now in generalized form, the inspiration still recognizable:

> *And women – things that live and move*
> *Mined by the fever of the soul –*
> *They seek to find in those they love*
> *Stern strength, and promise of control.*
>
> *They ask not kindness, gentle ways;*
> *These they themselves have tried and known:*
> *They ask a soul that never sways*
> *With the blind gusts which shake their own.*

(Perhaps we should emend 'blind gusts' to 'variable winds'.) Arnold had not had that strength to carry all before him; in a rare confession he tells us that from his childhood he had felt uncertainty, a lack of confidence in himself – perhaps from the dominance of that overwhelming father. He felt that, instead of piloting his own course, he was driven along, following his intuitions – for a poet, the better way. After the parting with Marguerite, a new Arnold emerges with marriage, family and a career, directing his own course: needs must.

> *Even so we leave behind,*
> *As, chartered by some unknown Powers,*
> *We stem across the sea of life by night,*
> *The joys which were not for our use designed,*
> *The friends to whom we had no natural right,*
> *The homes that were not destined to be ours.*

Then, in conclusion, in some of the most famous lines he ever wrote:

> *Who ordered that their longing's fire*
> *Should be, as soon as kindled, cooled?*
> *Who renders vain their deep desire? –*
> *A God, a God their severance ruled;*
> *And bade between their shores to be*
> *The unplumbed, salt, estranging sea.*

1 Dr Arnold, painted by T. Phillips in 1839

2 Matthew Arnold's grandfather,
the Rev. John Penrose

3 Matthew Arnold's mother,
Mary Penrose

4 Laleham church in Arnold's boyhood; photograph by Henry Taunt

5 Fox How, the Arnold home in the Lake District

6 Rugby Chapel by Radclyffe, *c.* 1840

7 Oxford from the 'Childsworth Farm' of *Thyrsis*

8 (*Right*) Balliol College in Arnold's time

9 Oriel College, St Mary's in the background

10 George Sand by J. L. Boilly,
c. 1840s

11 Arthur Hugh Clough, *c.* 1860

12 (*Right*) Matthew Arnold:
an Elliott and Fry photograph,
c. 1883

Some day I shall be cold, I know,
As is the eternal moonlit snow,
Of the high Alps, to which I go.

ON THE RHINE

13 Chamonix and Montblanc
   by Schnorr von Carolsfeld
   (1788–1853)

14 Hotel Bellevue,
   Thun, *c.* 1840

15 View of Thun
   by Gabriel Lory

16 The Cherwell at Oxford
17 Hinksey in the second half
of the nineteenth century

18 *The Signal Elm,*
that looks on Ilsley Downs
THYRSIS

19 Matthew Arnold:
H. Weigall's portrait in
the Athenaeum

20 James Holland's painting of
the Athenaeum Drawing Room

Mens Conscia.

Inspector (*who notices a backwardness in History*). "WHO SIGNED MAGNA CHARTA?"   (*No answer.*)

Inspector (*more urgently*). "WHO SIGNED MAGNA CHARTA?"   (*No answer.*)

Inspector (*angrily*). "WHO SIGNED MAGNA CHARTA!!!"

Scapegrace (*thinking matters are beginning to look serious*). "PLEASE, SIR, 'TWASN'T ME, SIR!!"

21 The school inspector by Charles Keene, 1860s

22 Matthew Arnold in later life

23 Tristram and Iseult in Cornwall

24 The Scholar Gypsy, from a 1900 edition of Arnold's poems

The affair, as these things go, had been brief – briefer than Shakespeare's; the consequences, as these things are apt to be, were enduring. Ten years later Arnold was in Switzerland again, happily married now, with his wife. It happened that his wife was unwell; so, as he paced the terrace at Berne, looking towards the Blümlis Alp with Thun and its lake not far away, he had his thoughts to himself and could write a poem.

> Ten years! – and to my waking eye
> Once more the roofs of Berne appear;
> The rocky banks, the terrace high,
> The stream – and do I linger here? . . .
>
> And from the blue twin lakes it comes,
> Flows by this town, the churchyard fair,
> And neath the garden-walk it hums,
> The house – and is my Marguerite there?
>
> Ah, shall I see thee, while a flush
> Of startled pleasure floods thy brow,
> Quick through the oleanders brush,
> And clap thy hands, and cry: 'Tis thou!
>
> Or hast thou long since wandered back,
> Daughter of France! to France, thy home;
> And flitted down the flowery track
> Where feet like thine too lightly come?
>
> Doth riotous laughter now replace
> Thy smile, and rouge, with stony glare,
> Thy cheek's soft hue, and fluttering lace
> The kerchief that enwound thy hair?
>
> Or is it over? – art thou dead? –
> Dead? – and no warning shiver ran
> Across my heart, to say thy thread
> Of life was cut, and closed thy span!

Evidently he had heard no further news of her, had completely lost touch; but we can tell from the verses that the man is still moved.

Could from earth's ways that figure slight
Be lost, and I not feel 'twas so?
Of that fresh voice the gay delight
Fail from earth's air, and I not know?

Or shall I find thee still, but changed,
But not the Marguerite of thy prime?
With all thy being re-arranged,
Passed through the crucible of time;

With spirit vanished, beauty waned,
And hardly yet a glance, a tone,
A gesture – anything – retained
Of all that was my Marguerite's own?

A married man, roped and tied, he did not go further to see, or even to inquire:

I will not know! – for wherefore try
To things by mortal course that live
A shadowy disability
For which they were not meant, to give?

He has arrived at philosophic consolation:

Like driftwood spars which meet and pass
Upon the boundless ocean-plain,
So on the sea of life, alas!
Man nears man, meets and leaves again.

I knew it when my life was young,
I feel it still, now youth is o'er!
The mists are on the mountains hung,
And Marguerite I shall see no more.

She had played out her part in his imagination, through which, in the poetry it gave rise to, she still lives.

CHAPTER 4

The Elementary School Inspector

THOUGH THE AFFAIR with Marguerite was over, the profound emotional disturbance of it continues to be reflected in his poems, directly in those that are frankly autobiographical, indirectly in others. It seems that the later 1840s and early 1850s produced most of his best poetry – a small span compared with Tennyson who continued to pour out good poetry (with bad) all his life. Two of Arnold's most beautiful poems clearly reflect the experience and the desolation in which it left him. 'A Summer Night' recalled

> *the same restless pacings to and fro,*
> *And the same vainly throbbing heart was there,*
> *And the same bright calm moon.*

> *And the calm moonlight seems to say –*
> Hast thou then still the old unquiet breast
> That neither deadens into rest
> Nor ever feels the fiery glow
> That whirls the spirit from itself away,
> But fluctuates to and fro
> Never by passion quite possessed
> And never quite benumbed by the world's sway?

There was the dilemma that had frustrated his affair with Marguerite and brought it to a stop. Now:

> *And I, I know not if to pray*
> *Still to be what I am, or yield – and be*
> *Like all the other men I see.*

We shall see that, a deeply conventional man as to morals – brought up in the embrace of that desperately moral middle-class family – he yielded, opted for a conventional career and became, to all intents, like the other men he saw around him, at least outwardly. The result is to be read in 'The Buried Life' – the very title has come to have a prophetic significance for others – with its famous lines:

> But often, in the world's most crowded streets,
> But often, in the din of strife,
> There rises an unspeakable desire
> After the knowledge of our buried life,
> A thirst to spend our fire and restless force
> In tracking out our true, original course.

What was his true original course? There can be no doubt about that: it was to be a poet, he should have sacrificed everything and everybody to fulfil himself as such. It was in composing that he felt himself happiest, and even confessed to 'cheerfulness' – an indication that here was his real nature. But, an athletic and masculine type – keen on walking, climbing, swimming, and even on drilling (as a volunteer reservist during the Crimean War) – there remained the sexual urge to satisfy and, being an Arnold and a Penrose, in a conventional way.

His brother Tom at this time said that Matt was the last person to think of as happily married. But Tom, the better classical scholar, had no judgment whatever, as witnessed by the perpetual shuttling to and fro in his career, and in his religious beliefs, until he finally fell into the arms of Newman. His was a wasted life, to the despair of his family – except that he produced a gifted daughter in Mrs Humphry Ward; and, as usual with a weakling, incapable of coping effectively with life, he has remained a favourite with the family.

It is obvious that Matt was aching to be married. And shortly there crossed his path a marriageable English girl whose grey-blue eyes seem to have reminded him of Marguerite:

> In this fair stranger's eyes of grey
> Thine eyes, my love, I see.

> *I shudder: for the passing day*
> *Had borne me far from thee.*

This was Frances Lucy – known to the family as Fanny Lucy – daughter of Judge Wightman. There was no doubt that she was a suitable marriage and shortly Matt was in love with her. With men, one love does not exclude another; and again there is no doubt that, when it came about, it was a genuine love-match, and the couple were happy with each other.

There was again a difficulty in external circumstances, but one that could be surmounted. Judge Wightman expected a prospective son-in-law to have a regular job sufficient to maintain wife and children. This held up the affair for a time – and again there is the deepest reserve and lack of information from Arnold about it. The family tradition is that he followed Fanny Lucy to the Continent, and the affair with her is similarly reflected in two famous poems. 'Calais Sands' was written in August 1850, and Arnold sent the first draft to her. He strains his eyes for the boat bringing her back across the Channel:

> *Thou comest! Yes, the vessel's cloud*
> *Hangs dark upon the rolling sea!*
> *Oh that yon seabird's wings were mine*
> *To win one instant's glimpse of thee!*
>
> *I must not spring to grasp thy hand,*
> *To woo thy smile, to seek thine eye;*
> *But I may stand far off, and gaze,*
> *And watch thee pass unconscious by.*
>
> *And spell thy looks, and guess thy thoughts,*
> *Mixed with the idlers on the pier.*
> *Ah, might I always rest unseen,*
> *So I might have thee always near!*

Later, when he had his wish, the scene is reflected from the other side of the Channel, in 'Dover Beach', with its often quoted conclusion – strangely despairing in the circumstances of a happy marriage:

Ah, love, let us be true
To one another! for the world, which seems
To lie before us like a world of dreams,
So various, so beautiful, so new,
Hath really neither joy, nor love, nor light,
Nor certitude, nor peace, nor help for pain.

While abroad on the Continent in the late 1840s Arnold began 'Tristram and Iseult', to complete it in England. It may be because of this that the poem so obviously falls into two parts: the third section with its story of Merlin and Vivien is really a separate poem. Arnold had been struck by an article by Villemarqué, an authority on Celtic subjects who studied and translated Breton legends and folklore. Arnold read the article at Thun, where the poem formed in his mind. Hence the Breton perspective of the poem. He was the first to deal with the theme, which was to prove such a fertile source of inspiration in nineteenth-century literature and art: not only with Tennyson, Swinburne and Thomas Hardy, but in music with Wagner, and in Pre-Raphaelite painting and tapestries. Tennyson, Swinburne and Hardy all took the trouble to come to Cornwall for its Arthurian associations, the indubitable background for the legends in part, and to grasp something of the evanescent atmosphere for their poems. Though Arnold went once and again to Brittany, and knew Wales and Ireland, it is sad that he never came back to Cornwall, after early childhood, whence so much of his own strain came. Stranger still that he should have been comparatively unaware of it – all the more so since he was drawn to Celtic subjects.

It would seem that there was more of Arnold's own situation, at least in imaginative sympathy, in Tristram's, caught between his loves for two women. And in Arnold's almost unparalleled way of playing about with his poems, deliberately altering their order, displacing them in different editions, concealing dates and covering his tracks, he curiously inserted a passage from another poem, which has nothing to do with Iseult's story:

Yes, now the longing is o'erpast

Which, dogged by fear and fought by shame,
Shook her weak bosom day and night,
Consumed her beauty like a flame . . .
Yet, were it lifted to the light,
The sweet expression of her brow
Would charm the gazer, till his thought
Erased the ravages of time,
Filled up the hollow cheek, and brought
A freshness back as of her prime.

Whose image is this, if not Marguerite's in Switzerland? – we know that she was languid and pale and drooping in that clime.

In 1850 Arnold's favourite sister, 'K' – after a previous unhappy love affair about which nothing is known – married the philanthropic Quaker, W. E. Forster, and went to the good with him: no children, nothing but good works all the way along. In order to marry Miss Wightman Matt had to settle for an inspectorship of schools to provide for his treasure: they were married on 10 June 1851. Sainte-Beuve said the last word on the matter: *Je connais Arnold, il nous aimait beaucoup dans sa jeunesse; il est allé voir George Sand à Nohant. C'est un français et un romantique égaré là-bas. Depuis, il s'est marié, s'est réglé, et dans ses poésies il reste fidèle au culte des anciens et de l'art. S'est réglé* may be translated, 'he settled down'; the rest says a great deal in a few words: it reads like an epitaph.

During these years Arnold expressed his innermost concerns of mind – not of heart – on poetry, religion, society to Clough, his closest intellectual companion. While both were in London, still bachelors, they continued their Oxford habit, breakfasting together twice a week. Having thrown over the charm of Oriel on account of the intolerable burden of the Thirty-Nine Articles on his sensitive conscience, Clough found University Hall in London no more satisfactory without the burden, was dismissed from the principalship in 1851 and departed for the United States, where one would have expected him to be more at home – he had the etiolated companionship of Emerson to support him.

Arnold did his best to find his difficult friend an inspectorship along with himself, to marry on. 'Hard dull work, low salary, stationariness, and London to be stationary in under such circumstances do not please me. However, I myself would gladly marry under any circumstances, and so, I doubt not, you feel.' It was as well that he had that consolation for what was, if he could have known it, a life-sentence. To his wife he wrote from Manchester, 'I think I shall get interested in the schools after a little time, their effects on the children are so immense, and their future effects in civilising the next generation of the lower classes, who, as things are going, will have most of the political power of the country in their hands, may be so important.' This was looking very far ahead, a whole century in fact; if he could have seen some of the consequences of mass-education – the uneducated in full pursuit of the uneducable – would he not have found reason for some disillusionment? He consoled his wife with, 'we shall certainly have a good deal of moving about; but we both like that well enough, and we can always look forward to retiring to Italy on £200 a year.' Alas, for his hopes! Where the Brownings must have had an income of £1,000 a year – and living in Italy was cheap – Arnold was always hard up and condemned to a life of incessant drudgery.

His inspectorate covered a great deal of the Midlands and Wales, and he was perpetually travelling about. This gave him a country-wide acquaintance with actual social conditions such as none of his fellow-writers had – neither Carlyle nor Ruskin, Tennyson, Thackeray nor even Dickens – but it took it out of him. It was a strain on his physical and mental energy; it is extraordinary to think what he managed to achieve and to write in these discouraging circumstances. At the end of his wedding year, from Birmingham: 'I have had a hard day. Thirty pupil teachers to examine in an inconvenient room, and nothing to eat except a biscuit, which a charitable lady gave me.' However, 'this is, next to Liverpool, the finest of the manufacturing towns: the situation high and good, the principal street capital, the shops good, cabs splendid, and the Music Hall unequalled by any Greek building in England that I have seen.' He should see the rebuilt centre of Birmingham today – hardly distinguishable from

Indianapolis or Big Bend, perpetual canned music laid on to fill the vacuity of mind of the idiot people: appalling!

To Clough he wrote, what he hardly could to his highminded family, the discouraging truth: 'I am more and more convinced that the world tends to become more comfortable for the mass, and more uncomfortable for those of any natural gift or distinction.' He went on to console himself – like the Liberal he was, 'but a Liberal not of the present but of the future' – with the reflection that 'it is as well perhaps that it should be so, for hitherto the gifted have astonished and delighted the world, but not trained or inspired or in any real way changed it.' This is again a young man's reflection, and it is not true; the Industrial Revolution was at that very moment changing the lives of the masses for the better, giving them more to eat, and enabling far more of them to survive. Gifted men like Peel and Cobden devoted themselves to cheapening the price of food to enable the masses to proliferate – as they did. Whether this is the ultimate test in history may be doubted: nothing of ordinary humans endures in history; they simply recur. What endures are the mighty achievements of elect spirits in art and the intellect, in science or even in religion.

To Clough he confessed sadly, 'how life rushes away, and youth. . . . What a difference there is between reading in poetry and morals of the loss of youth, and experiencing it! And, after all, there is so much to be done, if one could but do it.' We shall watch with admiration, if not altogether with sympathy for the impediments with which he loaded himself, the struggle he put up to accomplish something in his day and time. Actually, these were far from un-propitious to achievement, even if not so inspiring to poetry as the Elizabethan Age had been – but that was a miraculous moment, unique in our history. If Arnold considered Victorian England unpoetical, it was at least a country moving up in the world, with an expansive impulse, great energy and *essor*, not a down-at-heel society bent on sinking further down.

With Arnold it was the poetry that suffered, while he was con-stantly travelling, inspecting schools, examining dreary pupil teachers. For the first seven years of married life he hadn't a home of

73

his own. Often his wife accompanied him; their first child, Tom, was born, feeble and invalidish, in lodgings in Derby between the prison and the workhouse. Sometimes his wife and he took refuge for a time with her parents in Eaton Place; to make a little extra money, he would accompany his father-in-law, the Judge, as his marshal on circuit. To a friend, in July 1852: 'the baby is now squalling upstairs.' The joys of family life were beginning to close in upon him.

From Derby in October 1852 to a friend: 'I write this very late at night, with S——, a young Derby banker, *trés sport*, completing an orgy in the next room.' A little later: 'S—— is in a state of collapse. He will be very miserable tomorrow.' Here indeed was the average man. It was from here that Arnold looked towards Fledborough, recollecting 'the only approach I have to a memory of a golden age'. Even Rugby now had a glow upon it: 'I cannot tell how strange the feeling was of dining in the old house, in the very room where I used to sit after everyone was gone to bed composing my themes, because it was such a pretty room, it was a pleasure to sit up in it.' From Hampton to his mother on her birthday, 'for nearly thirty years such a mother as few sons have. The more I see of the world the more I feel thankful for the bringing up we had, so unworldly, so sound, and so pure.' We may reflect that it would have been better for his poetry if it had been less pure and moralistic, less cabined and confined and middle class.

Back to London for 'one of the most uncomfortable weeks I ever spent'. Incessant rain, execrable roads, and he could not afford to take a cab over Battersea Bridge. On to Cambridge: 'I have had a long tiring day, and it certainly will be a relief when I get these Eastern Counties over. The worst of it is that invitations to go and see schools are *rained* upon me; and managers who have held out till now against the Government plan ask me on my father's account to come and inspect them, and to refuse is hard.' He found it 'strange to be in a place of colleges that is not Oxford'. But he was received by a devoted pupil of his father's, whose picture hung in his room. This was John Gell, who carried Dr Arnold's mission to the Antipodes and became the founder of the public-school system of Tasmania. Gell took the Doctor's son all over Cambridge, 'yet I feel that the

Middle Ages and all their poetry and impressiveness are in Oxford, and not here.'

To his wife, from Suffolk: 'all this afternoon I have been haunted by a vision of living with you at Berne, on a diplomatic appointment, and how different that would be from this incessant grind in schools.' There was, however, never to be any relief from the incessant grind. From a school at Ipswich: 'I am too utterly tired out to write. It certainly was nicer when you came with me, though so dreadfully expensive; but it was the only thing that could make this life any-thing but positive purgatory.' He certainly paid a high price for the joys of family life.

In the midst of all this he produced his second volume, *Empedocles on Etna, and other Poems*, 'By A. 1852'. The volume contained some of his finest poems, in addition to the classical drama, its title-piece, remarkable on any account. It included 'Tristram and Iseult', a favourite poem with Arnold himself, most of the moving Marguerite pieces, and such fine poems as 'A Summer Night', 'The Buried Life' and 'Obermann'. The volume may be regarded, on the whole, as one of the best to appear in the century. It had a cold and unfriendly reception, was hardly noticed at all and, after a mere fifty copies had sold, Arnold withdrew it from publication as he had done its predecessor.

Reviews by third-rate reviewers are of no importance, but his friends were hardly any better. Here is Shairp: 'I fear Matt's last book has made no impression on the public mind. It does not much astonish me, for though I think there's great power in it, one regrets to see so much power thrown away upon so false and uninteresting (too) a view of life. Anything that so takes the life from out things must be false.'

Here we see the fallacy of a second-rate mind in criticism: Shairp, himself a minor versifier and a professor of poetry, cannot appreciate what he does not agree with. He proceeds to argue with the poetry; but poetry is not intended for argument, and not to be argued with. Real poetry arises from the heart and communicates itself to another heart that responds to it: that is the reflection with which Leslie

Stephen consoled Hardy, and a true poet in our time, Philip Larkin, comments that that is about all that needs to be said about poetry.

Arnold was deeply discouraged, as those who are unsupported by contempt for ordinary minds, if that is the word for it, are apt to be. He not only withdrew the volume but banished the title-piece from succeeding volumes for years, until prevailed upon by Browning to reinstate it. Not until 1867 did he do so – 'at the request of a man of genius, whom it had the honour and the good fortune to interest'. There is a reproof in those words, as well as politeness: Browning was a man of genius, others were not. Even the response of Clough, a man of uncertain and fitful genius, was uncertain and fitful, cool and ungenerous from a friend.

Arnold had continued to impart his inmost projects to his friend, as he had lent him money, out of the little enough he could spare: 'nothing would please me more than for you to make use of me, at any time, as if I were your brother.' He wrote testimonials for his senior, hopeless at holding down a job. He suggested literary projects to him, which reveal his own mind and foreshadow future work. He suggested (1) 'an edition of the Greek lyric poets before Sophocles that should be *readable*'. Instead of the book being cluttered up with pedantic references it should be presented and annotated in English, 'as if you were writing a book for educated persons interested in poetry to read. Every fragment should be followed by its literal prose translation. (2) The same for Theocritus and his contemporaries' – precisely such a plan to follow as with the Sonnets of Shakespeare, for example: a modern edition, with introduction and notes, each sonnet followed by its literal prose version. It is only common sense that a book should consider the reader and be designed to be read. Matthew Arnold was not a first-class classical scholar, but the greatest classical scholar of our time, A. E. Housman, also a poet, says, 'when it comes to literary criticism, heap up in one scale all the literary criticism that the whole nation of professed scholars ever wrote, and drop into the other the thin green volume of Matthew Arnold's Lectures on Translating Homer, and the first scale, as Milton says, will straight fly up and kick the beam.'

This is excessively generous of Housman, who detested the

second rate; but one of the qualities of genius, which Arnold possessed, was an inspired and practical common sense. This Clough had not. Others of Arnold's suggestions of work for Clough had life and sense in them: to translate the biographies of Diogenes Laertius, leaving out the trash and presenting them as 'living biographies so far as they go'; to carry on Johnson's Lives of the Poets from where he ended. Clough took up none of these practical projects; the last of them was ultimately carried out by Humphry Ward, with a Preface by Arnold.

It is in the letters to Clough that we have Arnold's critical convictions (and prejudices) stated in simple, forthright manner, foreshadowing his later more professorial statements in lectures, essays, prefaces. In 1852 he is already committing himself to the doctrine of greater plainness of style, as against the romantic exuberance and richness coming down from the Elizabethans. 'Critics cannot get to learn this, because the Elizabethan poets are our greatest, and our canons of poetry are founded on their works.' Arnold was on surer ground when he went on to emphasize the primacy of composition – in which he thought all Northern art inferior to Mediterranean; he meant putting the conception of the work as a whole before the detail, and subordinating the latter to the former. All this was an implied rejection of Tennyson, whose extraordinary popularity dominated the idea of what poetry was to most Victorians. Arnold aligned himself with the plain speech, as well as much of the ideas, of Wordsworth. Wordsworth had never been a popular poet, neither was Arnold. He occasionally reflects sadly how little his poetry appealed to the public; he was a poet for the few, practically to the end of his life. Discouraging as this was, it was still more so that his friends understood him little better.

Easily cast down, he was his own severest critic, sometimes going the length of condemning his own best work, the inspired 'Scholar Gipsy', for example. His doctrine of plainness of speech did not help: it was really an extrapolation of his own defect – as is often the way with criticism (notoriously with Leavis's, for example): the erection of the critic's own defects into 'objective' doctrine. Arnold had a defective ear, no ear for music whatever – unlike Tennyson; making a doctrine out of his own bareness of expression, with its reiterated 'Ah's' to fill up the line, and superfluous exclamation marks to enforce an emotion inadequately expressed, made his poetry still less attractive to the discerning reader. Doctrine is liable to lead poets, indeed all artists, astray; he answers his own with the quatrain:

> *What Poets feel not, when they make,*
> *A pleasure in creating,*
> *The world, in its turn, will not take*
> *Pleasure in contemplating.*

Actually in 1853 Arnold was engaged on the poem which gave him much pleasure to write, 'Sohrab and Rustum'. 'All my spare time', he wrote to his mother, 'has been spent on a poem . . . which I think by far the best thing I have yet done, and that it will be generally liked – though one can never be sure of this. I have had the greatest pleasure in composing it – a rare thing with me and, as I think, a good test of the pleasure what you write is likely to afford to others; but then the story is a very noble and excellent one.' When it came out in the new volume of 1853, the leading piece, 'Clough, as usual, remained in suspense whether he liked it or no. . . . I am worked to death just now, and have a horrid cold and cough.' The Arnolds were moving into Eaton Place with the Judge for a couple of winter months, he hoped, to save expense. Next summer they could afford only a brief visit to Belgium: 'I have so little money this year that I really could not have afforded to spend more than what I have spent on travelling.' No holidays abroad this year, or 'I should have been more embarrassed than ever on my return.'

From the other side of the Atlantic came reproaches from Clough that Arnold had grown cold towards him. Arnold defended himself with a frank explanation, so far as so reserved a man could. Clough had been annoyed once or twice in London, 'but at that time I was absorbed in my speculations and plans and agitations respecting Fanny Lucy, and was as egoistic and anti-social as possible. People in the condition in which I then was always are . . . being in love generally unfits a man for the society of his friends.' Conventionally heterosexual as Arnold was, emotional warmth in him seems to have gone towards women and to his family. He condemned himself of coldness and want of robustness, though Clough's company always had 'a charm and a salutary effect for me. . . . I cannot say more than that I really have clung to you in spirit more than to any other man.' Summing up their relationship, 'I do not think we did each other harm at Oxford. I look back to that time with pleasure. . . . If you had never met me, I do not think you would have been the happier or the wiser on that account: though I do not think I have increased your stock of happiness. You have, however, on the whole, added to mine.' Later, Arnold confessed that he cared more for what Clough thought about his work than anyone else; Clough was less responsive on that subject, or could not make up his mind, as usual.

Clough had asked his junior for his opinion 'in what I think or have thought you going wrong. In this: that you would never take your *assiette* as something determined, final and unchangeable for you, and proceed to work away on the basis of that; but were always poking and patching and cobbling at the *assiette* itself – could never finally, as it seemed, "resolve to be thyself".' Arnold put his finger on the source of the trouble with Clough – what I have called, for ever pulling up the roots to see how they were getting on. This is fatal to creative work, which requires a secure reliance on intuition (Shakespeare is the great exemplar) and not too much exposure of the process of creation to the arc-lamp of self-conscious criticism: the criticism comes afterward, not to be mixed up with the process of creation.

That Arnold was aware of this we know from a later letter: 'I can feel, I rejoice to say, an inward spring. . . . But of this inward spring one must not talk, for it does not like being talked about, and threatens to depart if one will not leave it in mystery.' All poets instinctively know this to be true.

It is doubtful whether any such *éclaircissement* does any good between friends. However, for his part, Arnold continued to confide in Clough – the hopes he had of 'Sohrab and Rustum', though 'it is pain and grief composing with such interruptions as I have.' In reviewing the poem Clough took exception to one or two lines that reminded him of Tennyson, and for the rest was cool enough. Poor

Matt!: 'but never mind – you are a dear soul. I am in great hopes you will one day like the poem – really like it. There is no-one to whose *aperçus* I attach the value I do to yours – but I think you are sometimes – with regard to *me* especially – a little cross and wilful.'

Who was the generous one in this relationship – the one of greater, or the one of lesser, genius? Clough was lucky to be commemorated in 'Thyrsis', one of the finest elegies in the language.

This lack of appreciation was nothing compared with what Arnold had to put up with from another old friend, John Duke Coleridge. A High Churchman, he wrote a crabbing review in the *Christian Remembrancer*, taking Arnold to task for his inadequate appreciation of the Deity in creating the works of nature. Worse, he made use of the personal information Arnold had given him as to the source of the poem to suggest that he was plagiarizing from the French on Firdusi. Here is an example of what a friend can do! A better Celt than Arnold, I should never have forgiven him; Arnold, a better Christian, 'was quick to forgive and forget the wrong'. He merely wrote to a common friend, 'my love to J.D.C., and tell him that the limited circulation of the *Christian Remembrancer* makes the unquestionable viciousness of his article of little importance.' To Coleridge Arnold took the trouble to defend himself – superfluously to a pedestrian mind – for imitating Milton: 'Tennyson is another thing; but one has him so in one's head, one cannot help imitating him sometimes. But, except in the last two lines, I had kept him out of "Sohrab and Rustum".'

The loyal Stanley took up the cudgels on his behalf. 'As a friend he [Arnold] has good ground for complaint, because the fact of friendship adds so greatly to the severity of the charges against him', and the 'sharpness derives a new edge from the reviewer's own personal knowledge. You have made use of knowledge which you derived solely from him, in bringing against him a charge, as if from your own discovery, without acknowledgement from the two French writers on Firdusi. . . . You might as well complain of Shakespeare's versification of Plutarch, and much more of Tennyson's versification of the *Morte d'Arthur*.' Arnold continued to be friends with Coleridge as if nothing had happened; he was a gentleman to the core of his being, and really a more Christian spirit than the High Church lawyer – as we shall see from the Note-Books he began to keep, a kind of spiritual diary in which we see his soul laid bare. It was wiser of him not to resent the betrayal: he and Coleridge remained friends till death.

It remained for an historian, J. A. Froude, to do Arnold better justice; but Froude was a better prose-writer than any of them, and his admiration for the poetry did not prevent him from noticing subtler points which the professional *littérateurs* overlooked or were insensitive to. He wrote to Clough, 'Matt A.'s "Sohrab and Rustum" is to my taste all but perfect – I think he overdoes the plainness of expression which he so much studies, particularly in the beginning. And those repetitions of words (the word "tent" comes half-a-dozen times in the first 18 lines . . . certainly strikes an English ear unpleasantly). I don't think he studies enough the effect to be produced by the *sound* of words.' The historian had a finer ear than the poet, himself a good deal of a poet in prose. 'But the essentials – the working up of the situation is faultlessly beautiful.'

Froude went on to write a full-length article in the *Westminster Review* on all three of Arnold's volumes to date, giving an appreciative estimate of him as the outstanding and significant poet he was. Froude understood Arnold's classical aims as expressed in the Preface of 1853, which became a critical manifesto expanding the convictions he had confided to Clough. Even so, Froude could not help concluding, 'and yet it seems as if Teutonic tradition, Teutonic feeling, and Teutonic thought had the first claim on English and German poets'. Responsive to sympathetic suggestion, Arnold took the hint and next year wrote 'Balder Dead', based on the Norse Edda, though it turned out a more Homeric than Scandinavian saga.

The nineteenth century much overestimated everything German, and Froude, like most historians of the time, was a Teutonizer. So indeed Dr Arnold had been: he held Celts in the lowest estimation. We shall see how strongly his son reacted against this strain in the Victorian Age later, both in literature, with *The Study of Celtic Literature*, and politically, with his discriminating sympathy for the Irish point of view. A later letter tells us that Arnold had hoped to write a series of poems on the Nibelungenlied, the Teutonic cycle which Wagner used for his operas. A more tenacious scheme, of which some fragments and sketches remain, was that of a classic drama on Lucretius, which was to be his masterpiece. These poetic projects were sacrificed to what he called 'the dance of death in the elementary school'.

Froude's editorship of *Fraser's Magazine* meant that this distinguished periodical was open to the whole group of friends. Matt's youngest brother, William Delafield Arnold, now made his début in it with some articles on India, to which he had gone as a missioner for the Doctor's ideals. (When he first saw the Himalayas he was 'reminded of Papa'.) The experience of India made him reflect that 'I should have been a more useful active man had I never known the Truth as Papa taught it to us.' The slim young man with the mop of wavy black hair left Oxford without a degree because he was enjoying himself too much; joining the Army, he was scandalized by the language in the Mess and revolted by the immorality and squalor of the vast sump that was India. Moving over to education, he became Director of Public Instruction in the Punjab, where he laid the foundations of the educational system on non-sectarian lines. Ironically for a son of Dr Arnold, he prevented the imposition of Bible teaching as unjust to the Indians.

While on leave he wrote a novel, *Oakfield, or Fellowship in the East,* which also aroused controversy for its candid revelation of British ways in India. It was an exposure of the complacency which enabled the British shortly to be taken by surprise by the outbreak of the Indian Mutiny in 1857. After that, things were never quite the same. Nor was the book without its prophetic side, the hero's first glimpse of the scene registering 'the palm and the banyan tree, so alive with Oriental associations, speaking of a time ere yet that British power, now so manifest in all directions, had emerged from infancy in its own island cradle . . . apparently so firmly planted in the soil, and yet so manifestly separate from it; so that while it was impossible to fancy the power being swept away, it was easy to look round and think of it as gone' – as it has gone, and the sub-continent gone back to its indigenous chaos.

Like all the Arnolds, young Will could write – his disposition was that of his mother, with whom he was a favourite. Marrying young in India, he called his first son after the Penroses; three more children and his wife died. He himself died on his way home through the Mediterranean, only thirty-one: one of the innumerable sacrifices of life made for the benefit of India – to what point? His four children were adopted by the childless couple, Jane Arnold and W. E. Forster – hence the name Arnold-Forster; his grandson, Will Arnold-Forster, was the one member of the family to settle back in Cornwall, and from him I learned something of the family tradition.

Matt dedicated two fine poems to his brother's memory, 'A Southern Night', and, when he was in Brittany again, 'Stanzas Composed at Carnac'.

> *Ah, where is he, who should have come*
> *Where that far sail is passing now,*
> *Past the Loire's mouth, and by the foam*
> *Of Finisterre's unquiet brow,*
>
> *Home, round into the English wave? –*
> *He tarries where the Rock of Spain*
> *Mediterranean waters lave;*
> *He enters not into the Atlantic main.*
>
> *Oh, could he once have reached this air*
> *Freshened by plunging tides, by showers!*
> *Have felt this breath he loved, of fair*
> *Cool northern fields, and grass, and flowers!*
>
> *He longed for it – pressed on! – In vain.*
> *At the Straits failed that spirit brave.*
> *The South was parent of his pain,*
> *The South is mistress of his grave.*

It is notable that practically every one of Arnold's later poems is an elegy. What wonder, when so much of the energy of his mind went into the drudgery of his work, and much of his positive contribution to society in writing – Reports, essays, pamphlets, books of prose – his constructive work, was connected with it or related to it?

In 1846 the Privy Council had taken the first decisive step on the part of the state towards helping forward education. With the expansion of Victorian society in every sphere, the increase of resources and population, there was a continual increase in the number of schools set up by voluntary effort all over the country. There was no proper supply of teachers for them. The government stepped in with a grant to help to supply pupil teachers, i.e. senior scholars to help the schoolmasters. Inspectors were appointed to report on the schools and recommend grants according to merit, after examining them – something of this system remained in the elementary schools of my youth early this century. The inspectors were the key to the whole growing system, and a remarkable body of devoted men was built up – the most remarkable of them all Matthew Arnold, a unique figure among them, though other members of the Arnold-Penrose clan found their careers in this new sphere too.

The development of a national system of education was belated in England. We were decades behind France and Prussia – held up by sectarian conflict: chiefly, the furious jealousy of the Nonconformists – though they were split further into competing sects – of the Church of England and its schools, constantly hampering educational advance for their sectarian persuasions, perfectly willing to sacrifice the well-being of the children to their own desire for power and place under the name of religion. The leader of the Nonconformists in all this was the egregious Edward Miall, who vehemently campaigned all his life under the banner of 'the Dissidence of Dissent and the Protestantism of the Protestant Religion'. The expansion of the middle classes in the nineteenth century led to a large increase in the political power of Nonconformity, compared with the eighteenth century. There was not only this to contend with – there was the general Victorian belief in free enterprise, and a real hatred of state interference, even for the best causes. (Societies lurch from too much on one side to too much on the other: today immeasurably too much of the state and its bureaucracy, strangling free enterprise and initiative.)

Here was the background against which Arnold and his friends struggled all their lives, consistently, courageously, with justice of mind and a noble ideal to inspire them through all the drudgery and disappointment. Educational Bill after Bill was defeated in Parliament, there was incessant opposition to the idea of a national system of education, such as France and Prussia, even Holland, possessed. When the great Education Act of 1870, which founded a national system of elementary schools, was carried through Parliament by Arnold's brother-in-law, W. E. Forster, Miall and his friends opposed it tooth and nail. No wonder Miall and Miallism have such a place in Arnold's later essays in social criticism – the wonder is that he kept his temper with such a type, while privately detesting Nonconformity for its Philistinism and lack of cultivation.

Arnold, his family and friends, were deeply committed and involved in the struggle; and much as he disliked the *Zeitgeist*, they had the spirit of the age with them, ultimately the needs of a modern society prevailed, and they won – though not in the sphere of secondary education until fourteen years after his death. We must keep clear in our minds the work for elementary education carried forward as inspector all his life, and that for secondary education which he made his chief public campaign in his latter years. For all his complaints as to the drudgery his career in education involved, he was sustained not only by transparent devotion to duty but by an underlying enthusiasm for a cause, a dedicated idealism: his father came to win in him.

There was not only the support of the clan, but the friendship and loyalty of his superiors. This was much needed, for Arnold was very independent, and spoke out so courageously in public as to risk his career when the government took retrograde steps – as under the *laissez-faire* doctrinaire Lowe in 1862. He needed the support he got from two devoted officials in the Office: Lingen, who had been his tutor at Balliol, and Sandford, whom he had known there. They formed a little Balliol cell, to which the education of the expanding society owed so much. (Sandford's son married Arnold's daughter – the Viscountess Sandhurst, whom I met long ago in the house of one of the clan.) United, these devoted people ultimately won their battle.

We can read the progress of the campaign for the education of the people, year by year, in the Reports Arnold wrote to the Office during the thirty years 1852–82, which were published the year after his death. They make a wonderful book, the least known of all his works, beautifully written, crystal-clear and luminously persuasive. They form the chief of his general reports on the elementary schools in his inspectorate, with extracts from the dozen he wrote on the teachers' training colleges – he recognized from the first that educating the teachers was the indispensable foundation.

In his early years his area included one-third of England and Wales: hence the appalling amount of travelling about he had to undertake – though it gave him a larger and more concrete conspectus of the state of the country and of Victorian society than any of his fellow-prophets ever achieved. In his first year he visited 104 schools, all Nonconformist of different varieties: Church and Roman Catholic schools did not come within his province. The government grants covered schools for the lower middle classes and the upper crust of the working class, not the poorest. Arnold is always arguing for their inclusion. Working people paid 1d or 2d a week towards their children's schooling, though they could hardly afford it; naturally attendance was very irregular, and children were withdrawn to work from the age of nine or so. (This was the amount of education my parents enjoyed back in the 1860s, and both went to work at the age of nine – too many children to support, of course.) Arnold points out the truth: poor folk did not want education for their offspring, and never would, until it was made compulsory. He had to argue for twenty years before it was.

We will not concern ourselves with the detail of his reports, though these are very interesting. He comments on the uncleanliness of the London schools, the lack of ventilation, their insanitariness and the absence of playgrounds. He recommends white-washing, and constantly urges the provision of desks for the children – only one-third were provided for, the children had to rotate in their use. No wonder they were a lot of barbarous roughs who attended – no discipline in the homes; Arnold saw things improve, and was notably sympathetic and gentle in his treatment of children, as with his own. He comments on the extraordinary neglect of needlework among the lower orders – part of their general slatternliness, no doubt, though *he* does not say so. In Wales he was against Welsh-speaking in the schools: 'The children in them are generally docile and quick in apprehension to a greater degree than English children; their drawback is that they have to acquire the medium of information, as well as the information itself, while the English children possess the medium at the outset. . . . They are not the true friends of the Welsh people, who, from a romantic interest in their manners and traditions, would impede an event which is socially and politically so desirable for them.' An unexpected line from one so sympathetic to the Celtic element in literature, but education came first with him.

He was quick to see the advantage to society of the different conflicting sects having their children educated harmoniously in school together. He continually urged that, in the absence of a really national system, all was undetermined, subject to local variations and jealousies, and indeed to changes in policy at the centre. Such a drastic change came with Lowe's Revised Code of 1862, designed to cut back the growing expenditure on education, and to fix simply 'a minimum of education, not a maximum'. Lowe was not animated, as Arnold was, by the desire to improve the quality of education in the schools or 'to give those children an education that will raise them above their station and business in life'. This eminent Liberal drastically cut down the increasing expenditure through the grants-in-aid system, supervised by the inspectorate, in favour of payment by results based on an examination.

Arnold, though a mere civil servant in the employ of the Office, went all lengths in his opposition to the Revised Code. It was known in the Office that he was writing publicly against its new policy. The government's grant should be 'given to a school not as a mere machine for teaching reading, writing and arithmetic, but as a living whole with complex functions, religious, moral, and intellectual'. He saw the schools as civilizing influences towards improving the standards and cultivation of the lower classes in general. Through Forster, Arnold inspired the opposition in Parliament which made a successful breach in the retrograde Revised Code and modified it in detail.

To his mother he confided his vision of the future: 'The state has an interest in the primary school as a *civilising* agent, even prior to its interest as an *instructing* agent. When this is once clearly seen nothing can resist it, and it is fatal to the new Code. If we can get this clearly established in this discussion a great point will have been gained for the future dealings of the state with education, and I shall hope to see state-control reach in time our middle and upper schools.' What a prophet with a long range of vision – practical too – he was! For the moment, the important thing was to defeat Lowe and mitigate the damage he was doing. I think that the struggle aroused something of the fighter, his father's spirit, in him. From this time he ceased to be the bored and blasé young man he had affected to be: he became a campaigner and a propagandist for the rest of his life.

It was something to be the son of Dr Arnold; even when going against the official policy of his chief, and with his old patron, Lansdowne, distinctly cool, they could not touch him. 'I don't think, however, they can eject me,' he assured his wife, 'though they can, and perhaps will, make my place uncomfortable.' They did, for a bit; once or twice his Reports were returned for revision, they were so outspoken, and that for the regrettable year 1862 was suppressed. But they could not suppress *him*. He used his official missions to report on education on the Continent – assignments he welcomed with joy – to comment on the contrast and bring home the moral. In his first general report on the schools after four years, he said outright in 1867: 'I find in them, in general, if I compare them with their former selves, a deadness, a slackness, and a discouragement which are not the signs and accompaniments of progress. If I compare them with the schools of the Continent, I find in them a lack of intelligent life much more striking now than it was when I returned from the Continent in 1859. This change is certainly to be attributed to the school legislation of 1862.'

We note in this a new accent of authority. He had seen his opponent, and official superior, Lowe, off the pitch: he had been tripped up in Parliament and dispensed with as minister. And Arnold was within three years of seeing his brother-in-law carry through the revolutionary measure of 1870, which at last provided the country with a national system of primary education.

CHAPTER 5

The Professor of Poetry

ARNOLD'S ELECTION AS Professor of Poetry at Oxford in 1857 marked an epoch in his life as well as in that of that unduly publicized chair. He held it for two terms, for the ten years 1857 to 1867. With it he became for the first time a public figure in his own right, not just his father's son. His tenure of the chair made a golden age in its history; his godfather, Keble, had held it before him, a fair poet, but his lectures had been in Latin. Arnold's were in English and, creamed off in successive volumes, reached a much wider audience than the university to which they were addressed. The imprint of Oxford gave them a certain authority, people even objected to the *ex cathedra* air this gave them; they attained widespread notice, aroused much criticism as well as admiration, each volume stimulating controversy. Indeed, it is difficult to realize today, when we think of Arnold as the cool man he was, to what extent he irritated and annoyed the Victorians: he was a controversial figure – naturally for he was original, and did not think as others did.

Along with his poetry, which he was re-arranging and presenting with assiduity in the early 1850s, he was staking his claim to be the leading critic of poetry, taking the unusual step of equipping his volumes with critical prefaces. These were not only expositions of his aims, however unadmittedly defences of his poems, but also manifestos. He had the justification that poetic criticism was at an extremely low ebb at the time – the leading poet, Tennyson, though very much upset by reviewers, never bothered to explain himself but left his poetry to speak for itself. Arnold was more academic, and by nature and descent essentially didactic.

In 1853 he had brought out a new edition of his poems under his own name, mainly selected from his previous two volumes of 1849 and 1852, but omitting 'Empedocles on Etna' and explaining at length why. He now thought that a depiction of passive mental suffering which did not issue in action was painful, but not tragic. In his letters he even condemned his perfect poem, 'The Scholar Gipsy', because it did not 'animate' – a work of art must animate: what does it do for you? should be the test. It is doctrine chiefly that leads poets astray: they should follow their intuition, safer and subtler, as the great exemplar of poetry in the language always did. In his Preface Arnold criticized Shakespeare for 'curiosity of expression', 'an irritability of fancy, which seems to make it impossible for him to say a thing plainly'. This is obviously not so: Shakespeare could state things plainly enough, his imagination also bore him to the limits of expression of which the language was capable. Arnold's preference for classical plainness was in origin an extrapolation of his own thinness and limitedness of imagination.

We need not go into Arnold's defence of his choice of classical *subjects*, where he was on strong ground, though his argument did not demand that they should be held superior to modern themes: his argument in itself pointed to their equal consideration, they were *in pari materia*: the suitability and effectiveness of the subject in itself were what mattered. We may add a rider to this. In his time, when most cultivated people had received a classical education at school and university, the themes of the tragedy of the House of Atreus, of Iphigeneia, or Aeneas and Dido, were not only familiar but had reverberations of their own. Today, with the decline of classical education, they mean little to us. This is still no argument against them as subjects for art: it merely means that they have less appeal. Arnold's reiterated argument in favour of his classical subjects was unanswerable: it is the effect upon his own work that is in question. One realizes now that his constant girding against decorative detail was inspired by disapproval of Tennyson. Actually, Tennyson was something of a King Charles's head with Arnold, he loomed so large on the horizon – as Wells said of Henry James, Tennyson 'bothered' Arnold. As a poet he would have done better to learn from him: his own plainness of style became plain baldness, at worst not even poetry.

In 1854 a second edition of his Poems appeared, in which he republished the Preface of the year before, adding an Advertisement. In this he said, 'sanity – that is the great virtue of the ancient literature: the want of that is the great defect of the modern, in spite of all its variety and power.' He thought there was a morbid strain in Tennyson, as indeed there was, accentuated by his Pre-Raphaelite following; and Arnold disapproved of such a work as 'Maud'. But what of it? We see that Arnold's test was essentially moral, rather than aesthetic, which must have primacy in the realm of art. What would he have thought of Baudelaire and *Les Fleurs du Mal*, prosecuted for immorality in the year Arnold became Professor? It is doubtful if he knew the work – though his disingenuous friend, Sainte-Beuve, could have informed him – of a finer artist than himself, with a wider *retentissement* and a far deeper influence, both poetic and critical, in European literature. (Arnold never lectured on *him*, but on minor lights like Joubert, Senancour, Maurice and Eugénie de Guérin – academicism in the less admirable sense.)

In 1855 Arnold published his *Poems: Second Series*, led off by a new long narrative piece, 'Balder Dead'. He considered that this would 'consolidate the peculiar sort of reputation I got by "Sohrab and Rustum" '; he thought at the time of writing it that the new poem was superior. The family at Fox How thought otherwise, and they were right. It was not an inspired poem, for the poet's emotions were in no wise engaged. They had been deeply, if unconsciously, engaged in 'Sohrab and Rustum'; the whole tragedy therein lay in the relation between son and father. The father kills the son; only at the moment of death do they recognize each other, and what each has done to each. A transformation in psychological awareness – not the least of the revolutions in our century – has taken place between us and the Victorians: they were largely incapable of recognizing their own motivations (Gladstone is the most notorious exemplar). We need say no more, except that Arnold may not have realized why 'Sohrab and Rustum' is an inspired poem, while 'Balder Dead' is not.

We need not hold it against this poem that it depicts an exceedingly uncongenial, positively rebarbative world derived from the Norse

Edda, though it has its rather ludicrous side – the Nornies and god-desses called Nanna, and such. Arnold's addiction to the Homeric repetition of proper names and double epithets has betrayed him here, as elsewhere. The best poetic passages, the extended Homeric similes describing mountain scenery, are inspired by his passion for Switzerland. There are no less than five, all recognizable, of this character:

> *as when cowherds in October drive*
> *Their kine across a snowy mountain pass*
> *To winter pasture on the southern side,*
> *And on the ridge a wagon chokes the way,*
> *Wedged in the snow; then painfully the hinds*
> *With goad and shouting urge their cattle past,*
> *Plunging through deep untrodden banks of snow . . .*

And so on – even the storks of Switzerland appear.

In 1857 he published the third edition of his Poems, reprinting both the earlier Preface and Advertisement. The section 'Switzerland' was expanded to eight poems, and – as late as this – there is a new one, 'To Marguerite'. Strangely for one who was happily married, with a growing family of children he adored, the message is the essential solitariness of the human soul; but then, it is in the recesses of the imagination, not the external accompaniments of life, that the truth is told:

> *But thou hast long had place to prove*
> *This truth – to prove, and make thy own:*
> Thou hast been, shalt be, art, alone.

Those things that touch the soul

> *are unmating things –*
> *Ocean, and Clouds, and Night, and Day . . .*
> *And life, and others' joy and pain,*
> *And love, if love, of happier men.*
>
> *Of happier men – for they, at least,*
> *Have* dreamed *two human hearts might blend*

In one, and were through faith released
From isolation without end
Prolonged, nor knew, although not less
Alone than thou, their loneliness.

The essential isolation of the human spirit – there was Arnold's deepest conviction; it is evident that only religion could help him, and there the indispensable element of faith was wanting.

The suggestion here that the union of two souls was a dream is corroborated by yet another Marguerite poem, 'A Dream', of 1853. He was sailing with a friend down 'a green Alpine stream', when

On the brown rude-carved balcony two Forms
Came forth – Olivia's, Marguerite! and thine.
Clad were they both in white, flowers in their breast;
Straw hats bedecked their heads, with ribbons blue
Which waved, and on their shoulders fluttering played.
They saw us, they conferred; their bosoms heaved,
And more than mortal impulse filled their eyes.
Their lips moved; their white arms, waved eagerly,
Flashed once like falling streams. We rose, we gazed:
One moment, on the rapid's top, our boat
Hung poised – and then the darting River of Life,
Loud thundering, bore us by.

It had been a dream:

us, burning Plains
Bristled with cities, us the Sea received.

In 1857, too, Arnold was impelled to write his perhaps too famous tribute to his father, 'Rugby Chapel', which had a widespread appeal on account of the subject and the legend, rather than for the poem itself. The metre is unrhymed and uncongenial, and, though there is unstinted admiration, there is no love in it. Much of Arnold's work consisted of elegiac tributes to all kinds of people; perhaps it is significant that this one was called out only by reflections on his father's memory by one of the Cambridge tribe of Stephen. Arnold wrote to his mother, custodian of the prodigious Memory, 'it was Fitzjames Stephen's thesis of Papa's being a narrow bustling fanatic which moved me first to the poem. I think I have done something to fix the true legend about Papa, as those who knew him best feel it ought to run.' Already an historic figure, the Doctor would still have been only sixty-two if alive.

The poem begins with its best stanza, evoking nostalgically the playing fields of Rugby:

> *Coldly, sadly descends*
> *The autumn evening. The Field*
> *Strewn with its dank yellow drifts*
> *Of withered leaves, and the elms,*
> *Fade into dimness apace,*
> *Silent – hardly a shout*
> *From a few boys late at their play!*

And where was the Doctor now, that elemental force?

> *O strong soul, by what shore*
> *Tarriest thou now? For that force,*
> *Surely, has not been left vain!*
> *Somewhere, surely, afar,*
> *In the sounding labour-house vast*
> *Of being, is practised that strength,*
> *Zealous, beneficent, firm!*

The elusive son sounds unsure; but then he had never had the father's faith to uphold him; for all its anxiety to urge something positive, the poem expresses a sense of desolation.

The poet exhibits more energy in his expression of contempt for the purposelessness of ordinary people's lives – *there* was a contrast with his dynamic parent:

> *What is the course of the life*
> *Of mortal men on the earth? –*
> *Most men eddy about*
> *Here and there – eat and drink,*

> *Chatter and love and hate,*
> *Gather and squander, are raised*
> *Aloft, are hurled in the dust,*
> *Striving blindly, achieving*
> *Nothing; and then they die –*
> *Perish; and no one asks*
> *Who or what they have been . . .*

There is feeling enough, conviction at this point in the poem; and the contrast with the elect few:

> *And there are some, whom a thirst*
> *Ardent, unquenchable, fires*
> *Not with the crowd to be spent,*
> *Not without aim to go round*
> *In an eddy of purposeless dust . . .*
> *Ah yes, some of us strive*
> *Not without action to die*
> *Fruitless. . . .*
> *We, we have chosen our path –*
> *Path to a clear-purposed goal.*

This speaks for Arnold himself; he goes on to salute his father as a beacon along the hard mountain ascent the elect few have to climb. For all his calling in religion at the end to redress the balance of the poem, it is a pretty cool, objective, almost impersonal work for an elegy – not the inspired poem that 'Thyrsis' was to be, in memory of Clough. It is remarkable, too, how little Arnold mentions his father in all his voluminous writings on education – it is chiefly to his mother that he ever writes about 'Papa', evidently to please her; for to her he was devoted all his life.

Next year, 1858, he published his classical tragedy, *Merope*, again with a long critical Preface. He had been writing it all the time he could spare for composition in 1856–57, and reported that 'she is calculated rather to inaugurate my Professorship with dignity than to move deeply the present race of *humans*.' For all his professions Arnold was more ambitious, as with all his work: he tried to get the piece acted on the stage and to persuade a leading actress to undertake the part. If only Rachel, whose acting he worshipped, could have performed it! – no doubt he imagined her as Merope in writing the play.

Arnold's 'humans' never have responded to the work, either at the time or since; but, in fact, it is a finer piece than is generally realized – it is usual to dismiss it from his work, unread – while the long Preface, expounding his views of Greek tragedy and the treatment of the subject of European literature, is one of the most illuminating critical essays he ever wrote, far superior to better-known ones such as those on Shelley and Byron. Surprisingly, Arnold shows that he had dramatic sense – less surprising, when one considers his earlier addiction to the theatre. The speeches, though too long, are moving; where the play falls down is in the part played by the Chorus. Here, once more, it is doctrine that betrays the poet. Arnold was anxious to reproduce the effect of the Chorus in Greek tragedy in commenting on the action as it proceeds, and even went so far as to imitate the exact form, with strophe, antistrophe, etc. This reproduction is fatal to the drama – with its repetition of confirmatory platitudes at regular intervals even ludicrous in its effect – as the strong common sense of Dr Johnson, rarely at fault, perceived that such modern imitations of ancient practice were.

Johnson cited the chorus in *Samson Agonistes* against Milton, but it is more effective there than it is in Arnold's *Merope*. George Henry Lewes, the most sympathetic critic of the work, said that it was a pity that Arnold employed his gift in imitating, instead of creating, a work. One is bound to agree with him – and yet, with the Chorus much reduced, one would like to see the piece given its chance on the stage, possibly the finest example of its kind after *Samson Agonistes*. The Preface one cannot praise too highly: it ranges, in loftiness of reading and reflection, over the peaks of both Greek and modern tragedy, Maffei, Voltaire, Alfieri, Goethe – an eagle's view; it is even amusing on the subject of Aaron Hill. One sees that, of all Victorian writers, Arnold was the best European and had the widest culture. (He considered Tennyson provincial – but the provincial was the greater poet.)

With these volumes the bulk of Arnold's *oeuvre* in verse was completed: the prose-writer was to take over. (With this the paternal strain comes to the fore: he told his mother that pamphleteering was the *one* literary side he got from his father.) He published only one more volume of verse in the remaining thirty years of his life, a slim volume to celebrate the end of his Professorship in 1867; even that had few new poems in it. But we appreciate how careful he was of his poetic reputation, arranging and re-arranging, omitting and re-instating, with Prefaces and notes to give the best possible presentation of himself to the age. Though never a popular poet, he thought that his time would come – as it did; the best of his poetry lasted better than that of any of his contemporaries, except Tennyson, and won him his permanent place in our literature. Not his criticism.

Oxford offered Arnold not only a podium but a pulpit from which to preach, of which he took full advantage. If the moral element bulks displeasingly large in his lectures and essays in criticism, we must make allowance for the perspective of the Victorians who turned everything into ethics. It seems that they could not take a subject neat without regurgitating it as morals: economics, politics, aesthetics were all turned into ethics. So, as literary critic, Arnold was much of a moralist, with pronouncements such as that poetry was 'a criticism of life' bandied to and fro, discussed *ad nauseam* – as it still continues to be, as if it had any meaning.

From this time Arnold became known for launching these phrases into public discussion; Disraeli complimented him upon them, they stirred up the public and made it think, said the courteous old cynic. (Arnold, though a liberal, much preferred him to Gladstone.) Some of his phrases and categories have remained a permanent part of our intellectual baggage – Philistines and Philistinism, for example, which he took over from Heine. The repetition of these phrases in his printed work, perhaps an effective trick at the time, reads like a wearisome *tic* today. One sympathizes with Leslie Stephen, who wished that he had 'sweetness and light' so that he could say such nasty things about his enemies.

However, when one remembers the low state of literary criticism at the time, one sees how salutary Arnold's work was in this sphere and how much he did to improve it. All the more so for the tone and style he introduced into these academic forays: lightness and clarity, no pomposity, above all no philosophic pretensions to profundity. There was even a certain amount of banter – Oxford brought back the youthful Arnold. He was also very topical: he would often take up something from the newspapers of the day and make it his point of departure for a critical disquisition. He kept up a running campaign against his detractors, particularly of *The Times* and the *Saturday Review* – in fact, he made the running, and this made him news: a public figure at last.

Practical good sense was his aim in criticism, not philosophical discussion or linguistic hair-splitting. He announced in his first lectures the common-sense objectives of criticism: 'to know the best that has been known and thought in the world'; 'to see things as they are'; to regard matters with a certain detachment, to seek *disinterestedness* – which he underlined – to aim at justice of mind. There is, of course, no absolute attainment of such objectives, and they can go on being unprofitably discussed for ever; but one can at least try to advance along these lines. In his too much discussed lecture, 'The Function of Criticism at the Present Time' – his blueprint for the future, as it were – he says, 'a polemical practical criticism makes men blind even to the ideal imperfection of their practice, makes them willingly assert its ideal perfection, in order the better to secure it against attack; and clearly this is narrowing and baneful for them.'

How still more apposite that stricture is to literary criticism in our time – no conception, even, of justice of mind in such a critic as Leavis; when a more scholarly mind such as C. S. Lewis thought that English poetry had reached its term with Chesterton, because this view coincided with his prejudices; and even Eliot could hardly do justice to Milton and Shelley, because the one was a republican and the other an atheist; while the inanity of Auden on the subject of Tennyson, or many about Kipling, is unworthy of respect. The golden rule in criticism is catholicity of appreciation, and to be able to offset one's prejudices. Arnold himself could not keep up to his own declared standards: he underrated Shelley because of the confusion and disarray, the sheer silliness of much of his life: 'what a set! what a world!', the respectable middle-class Arnold wrote. One must set aside prejudice: the fact that Milton's political views were largely doctrinaire nonsense does not displace him from being the second poet in the language, after Shakespeare, whose reflections on society and politics make profound sense. Again one may not much care for Milton as a man – but that is neither here nor there. To be constructive, judgment in all matters of art must be an aesthetic one.

Arnold never forgot that 'the critical power is of lower rank than the creative' – the critic should therefore know his place. If he did not, there was Wordsworth, himself 'a great critic', to inform him with trenchant common sense: 'if the quantity of time consumed in writing critiques on the works of others were given to original composition, of whatever kind it might be, it would be much better employed; *it would make a man find out sooner his own level.*'

In a second lecture that occasioned much criticism, 'The Literary Influence of Academies', Arnold remarked that 'genius is mainly an affair of energy, and poetry is mainly an affair of genius; a nation whose spirit is characterized by energy may well be eminent in poetry – and we have Shakespeare.' But criticism demands intelligence: 'how much greater is our nation in poetry than prose! how much better, in general, do the productions of its spirit show in the qualities of genius than in the qualities of intelligence!' He went on to ask, 'why is all the *journeyman-work* of literature so much worse done here than it is in France? . . . Hardly one amongst us, who knows French and German well, would use an English book of reference when he could get a French or German one; or would look at an English prose translation of an ancient author when he could get a French or German one.'

This kind of thing, thoroughly justified and salutary as it was for mid-Victorian Oxford, infuriated the complacency of the Victorians, with their country at its apogee of power in the world, also assuming that it was at the apex of civilization. That place, in Arnold's view, was occupied by France. Nothing was more irritating to the Victorian English, who despised France, and were more favourably inclined to the less civilized Germans. What made his offence worse was that he was in fact unfair to the English. Applying his own standard, he asked, 'how much of current English literature come into this "best that is known and thought in the world"?' He answered, 'Not very much, I fear; certainly less, at this moment, than of the current literature of France or Germany.' This was hardly fair to the country that, at the moment, could put forth Tennyson, Browning, Arnold himself; Dickens, Thackeray, George Eliot; Carlyle, John Stuart Mill, Ruskin, Newman; Macaulay, Hallam, Froude.

Henceforth Arnold became a much-attacked man, as the original Preface to his *Essays in Criticism* states. He was accused of being un-English – as he was. His cultural sympathies were with the French – he was at his happiest in Paris; he was undoubtedly supercilious about his own countrymen, and unnecessarily depreciative of his fellow-writers. We have seen that he had something of a complex about Tennyson; though he got on with Browning, he did not much care for his poetry; he had no very high opinion of Dickens, and could not stand Ruskin; John Stuart Mill and Bentham he disapproved of, and derided Millism along with Miallism. And so on . . . I fear he was very finicking and hard to please – un-English in short. If one asked whom he admired unreservedly, though not uncritically, among the spirits of his age, one would have to say George Sand, Sainte-Beuve, Renan; Senancour, Joubert, Amiel; Heine and Rachel. It is a cosmopolitan list, strikingly un-Victorian; and he much enjoyed Jewish society, the Rothschilds and Disraeli, for their cultivated intelligence.

His aim was deliberately to challenge Victorian complacency; very much of a gadfly, he set himself to puncture the hide of a people intolerably pleased with themselves – as cultivated visiting Americans, Adamses, Jameses, Nathaniel Hawthorne, observed. In return, he aroused the fury of the favourite organs of Philistinism, as he put it: *Times* and *Telegraph*, *Saturday Review* and *Spectator*, above all, the organs of middle-class Dissent. All this had an effect on the public estimation of him in his own time: he was not only not a popular author – which he rather resented – but he was not properly appreciated at his true worth until after his death. In contemporary notices of him one observes a note of reserve, a question-mark, as if they did not know how to take him – as they did not; and not even in our time has there been any proper conception of what he achieved for the country in education.

Of course, we in our turn can criticize the critic. Since he was so appreciative of French culture, why did he not turn the attention of the English public to writers vastly more important than the Guérins, Joubert or Amiel? – To Sainte-Beuve or Renan, both of whom he knew; Victor Hugo (whom again he disliked), Lamartine or Alfred de Vigny, with whose spirit he had something in common; Balzac, or Flaubert or Baudelaire (but of these he would have disapproved).

The subjects he chose were highly moralistic: 'Pagan and Medieval Religious Sentiment', Marcus Aurelius, Spinoza, Joubert and Amiel (whom his niece, Mrs Humphry Ward, translated). One may take exception to a number of his dubious, too summary generalizations, historical or literary – as when he tells us that the Russians have never yet produced a great poet, or dismisses the English prose-writers of the eighteenth century. However, as a challenge to English self-satisfaction he was unmatched in his age. 'Remembering Spinoza's maxim that the two great banes of humanity are self-conceit and the laziness coming from self-conceit, I think it may do us good, instead of resting in our pre-eminence with perfect security, to look a little more closely why this is so, and whether it is so without any limitations.' Invariably there follow some home truths.

Arnold's lectures 'On Translating Homer' produced a controversy of a different sort. Since educated persons in those days were brought up on the classics, and Greek to them meant essentially Homer, many people were interested in the question how best to translate him. A number of persons were stimulated to reply to the Professor, who answered with 'Last Words on Translating Homer'. Tempers were easily raised on this riveting issue – as has been said, with some exaggeration, 'odium theologicum is nothing compared with odium archaeologicum.' The technical aspects of the dispute are of little interest to a Greekless age, but the general questions involved in translation from one language to another remain important.

Arnold began, 'it has more than once been suggested to me that I should translate Homer. That is a task for which I have neither the time nor the courage; but the suggestion led me to regard yet more closely a poet whom I had already long studied, and for one or two years the works of Homer were seldom long out of my hand.' We have noted the primary influence of Homer in his own narrative poems. Arnold was not an exact scholar; but the greatest of classical scholars was above the pedants in judging him, though pointing out that Arnold could make mistakes. A. E. Housman asks, 'who are the great critics of the classical literatures, the critics with real insight into the classical spirit? They are such men as Lessing or Goethe or Matthew Arnold, scholars no doubt, but not scholars of minute or profound learning.'

Housman would approve of the tribunal to which Arnold appealed as proper judges in the matter: scholars, but those possessing poetic taste and feeling. Certainly not the public in general: let not the translator 'trust to what the ordinary English reader thinks of him: he will be taking the blind for his guide. . . . Let him ask how his work affects those who both know Greek and can appreciate poetry.' He proceeds to sum up the characteristics of the Homeric style: rapid, plain and direct, both in thought and expression, and lastly noble, something grand in the effect. It is obviously difficult to render all these together; and Arnold goes through the leading translations, Chapman, Dryden, Pope, Cowper, showing how each fails to reproduce one or other of Homer's distinguishing characteristics, and none achieved the combination of all four together. With some reflections on other contemporary efforts, Arnold turned his batteries on a foremost recent attempt, by Newman's brother, Francis W. Newman.

Francis Newman was a good technical scholar and an interesting writer; but he had a vein of eccentricity (he said that his brother never had any conception of truth from the time he was a boy). Because Homer was already archaic to the classical Greeks, Newman thought that to translate him into archaic ballad-form was the right idea. The effect was highly uncouth, and the bantering Arnold made fun of him and his *outré* words, 'eld', 'bragly', 'bulkin'. As for the verse, he called it doggerel, and treated the translator – who, unlike his brother, was no poet – superciliously. Upon this there was hullabaloo, for Francis Newman was an awkward customer, and gave almost as good as he got.

Dogged by the idea of reproducing the effect of Homer as nearly as possible, though he had admitted at the outset that 'no one can tell how Homer affected the Greeks', Arnold plumped for hexameters and took the opportunity to pay tribute to *The Bothie of Tobernavuolich*, which he had not cared for on its appearance. Several more people were now involved in the Homeric fray, Dr Maginn, Gladstone, James Spedding. Challenged to give examples of the treatment he recommended, the Professor (who hated the title) produced some hexameters of his own, which no more commended them to others. Spedding made the mistake of citing Tennyson's blank verse as Homeric; this gave Arnold a chance of shooting at a favourite target – Tennyson's style was anything but plain, he said, characterized by 'extreme subtlety and curious elaborateness of expression'. However, hexameters rarely 'go' in English: they are contrary to the natural rhythms of an accentual language, and Arnold's were no exception.

Among those alerted by the Homeric controversy was Arnold's cousin, Charles Penrose, who had been Headmaster of Sherborne and edited Demosthenes but had now fallen asleep in a Lincolnshire curacy. Arnold sent on his letter to Clough: 'certainly it shows much of his old vitality and cleverness, which I thought had been extinct.' Penrose had been aroused by the lectures, and scored off his famous cousin quite effectively: 'I do not think that if Homer himself were to come to life again in England he could translate a single book of his Iliad into English hexameters satisfactorily. There is a sing-song and monotony in them which is peculiarly wearying to my ear. . . . I have one more stone to shy at the English hexameter: it is almost impossible that any metre not of spontaneous English growth should be natural and straightforward enough to reproduce the characteristics of Homer which you so admirably define.'

Having shot his bolt, and said the last word on Homer, Charles Penrose nodded off to sleep again – it is fairly clear that the Penrose side of the family had not the push of the Arnolds. For all Matt's protestation of *ennui* and boredom, he displayed the energy which he associated with genius – no one else in the family to the same extent. At this time his brother, Edward Penrose Arnold, with whom Matt stayed at All Souls, was anxious to give up his inspectorship, which covered Devon and Cornwall. (If only Matt's had done!) In sending Charles Penrose's letter to Clough Matt added, somewhat ungraciously, 'tell Tennyson he is the last person on whom I should have dreamed of inflicting a volume of poems – but I have great pleasure in sending him anything of mine that he really wants to see. You need not add that I care for his productions less and less, and am convinced both Alfred de Musset and Henri Heine are far more profitable studies, if we are to study contemporaries at all.'

Among those stimulated by the fuss Arnold had raised about Homer was the eminent astronomer, Sir John Herschel, who proceeded to translate the *Iliad* into hexameters. Tennyson now took up his pen to express what he, with surer instinct, thought of the measure:

> *These lame hexameters the strong-winged music of Homer!*
> *No – but a most burlesque barbarous experiment.*
> *When was a harsher sound ever heard, ye Muses, in England?*
> *When did a frog coarser croak upon our Helicon?*

Arnold took this home to himself – a not unfair exchange for all his tilting at Tennyson, who had sent a gruff, but not unfriendly, message: 'tell Matt to give us more Forsaken Mermans and Scholar Gipsies, not those things', i.e. prose pamphlets.

Of his mother's family two of her brothers died in these years, John and Thomas Trevenen Penrose. John, who died at Langton by Wragby in 1859, had been Bampton Lecturer at Oxford and a prolific writer of theological and religious works. He wrote on the Truth of Christianity, on Human Motives, the Utilitarian Theory of Morals; once and again on Miracles in Proving the Truth of Revelation, on the Atonement, on the Divine Mind and the Doctrine of the Trinity. In spite of his evident dedication he never achieved any position in the Church; none of the family on either side did, in

Church or State, not even Matthew Arnold. They had no pull – things might have been different if the Doctor had lived, with his strong pull with the Whigs. As it was, Matt wrote of Uncle Penrose, 'though not a successful man – at least, not successful in proportion to his powers, and I suppose not successful in proportion to his wishes – he never seemed an unhappy man; and for that, whether it was self-command or real content, I always admired him.'

Uncle Trevenen Penrose, who had been born in the far-off days at Crannick, died at Coleby, Lincolnshire, in 1862. Arnold stayed with him there on his school-inspecting visits. Uncle Trevenen, too, produced a book, on the Pentateuch – to be put in the shade by Bishop Colenso's epoch-making work, which raised a furore hardly less than that by Darwin. To Colenso Arnold was curiously unfair in his essay, 'The Bishop and the Philosopher'. Within his own family – not until seven years of marriage had he a home of his own to 'unpack his portmanteau' in – a second son, Trevenen, was born in 1855. (The name was carried over into the Huxley family, upon a marriage of the two: Trevenen was a brother of Aldous and Julian Huxley.) There followed Richard Penrose Arnold, a daughter who was 'a fiend at nights', and the youngest, Basil, who died as a child of two.

No wonder Arnold complained of being constantly hampered and hindered in his work, and short of money. In May 1857 'we talk of going abroad . . . but what to do with the three children is too embarrassing. Else I have a positive thirst to see the Alps again, and two or three things I have in hand which I cannot finish till I have again breathed and smelt Swiss air.' (We must remember the smoky air and appalling fogs of Victorian London.) To Clough he confided, 'imagine a claim from Oriel for £30 for caution money. What on earth is to be done.'

No wonder he regarded his election to the Athenaeum as bliss: he looked forward 'with rapture to the use of that library in London'. No one made better use of it; his letters show how much he frequented the Club – one sees his sad shade there 'writing at a window in the great Drawing Room. . . . I look out upon the façade of the Senior United and the open place in front between that club and ours, and on the roofs and colonnades of the old Italian opera. The Park below the Duke of York's column is full of people waiting for the guns to fire, for the Peace was signed yesterday.' This was on a cloudless day in March 1856, the end of the Crimean War. Again, 'this Athenaeum is a place at which I enjoy something resembling beatitude.'

In 1863 we hear of his mother enjoying a visit at last to her native Cornwall. Matt was anxious to escape the Encaenia Luncheon, plus royalties, at Oxford; 'but if that old duck Edward had gone up to All Souls [he was a Fellow], I don't think I should have been able to resist. . . . It is now pouring. How you must be catching it in Cornwall! and the one consolation which I should have – that it is good for fishing – does not affect you. Still, with or without fishing, how I should like to be down with you in Cornwall!' A couple of years later she went back again. Matt wrote from Berlin, where he was on an official mission to report on higher education, 'Papa's name and work are very well known here. . . . How I wish we were all going to be at Penzance with you and Edward!'

Arnold's last course of lectures on 'The Study of Celtic Literature' attracted wider notice and more controversy than ever, for the subject touched on a sensitive nerve and had implications not only literary but cultural and quasi-political. Once more Arnold was reacting *against* something, and deliberately pitting himself against the cherished complacencies and assumptions of his countrymen. He regarded himself, oddly, as wholly English and wrote from the English point of view. Others did not: to Professor Walter Raleigh he was 'a well-bred, highly cultivated stranger'; he was thought of as 'a rather elusive figure, an alien in every group in which he moves, a member, but always with a difference'. Arnold himself confessed towards the end of his life, to the Americans: 'perhaps I have not – I will not say – flattered the patriotism of my own countrymen enough, but regarded it enough.' He certainly had not, at any point.

But he had a lot to put up with: there was not only the self-satisfaction of the Victorian upper and middle class, there was the positive Teutomania, the glorification of everything Germanic that ran all through their culture. The Teutonic cult of such as Carlyle and Kingsley has its ludicrous sides, but in fact it ruined a good deal of their work. More important, practically all the leading nineteenth-century historians, Freeman, John Richard Green, Stubbs, Froude, concentrated entirely on the Germanic origins of the English people and – a crushing example of Victorian unselfawareness – regarded the British simply as of unmixed Anglo-Saxon stock.

This had profound consequences upon public opinion, and directly in the political sphere. At the outset Arnold quoted *The Times* – the arcanum of middle-class Philistinism to him – on the Welsh and their Eisteddfod. 'The Welsh language is the curse of Wales. Its prevalence and the ignorance of English have excluded, and even now exclude, the Welsh people from the civilisation of their English neighbours. An Eisteddfod is one of the most mischievous and selfish pieces of sentimentalism which could possibly be perpetrated. It is simply a foolish interference with the natural progress of civilisation and prosperity. Not only the energy and power but the intelligence and music of Europe have come mainly from Teutonic sources. . . . The sooner all Welsh specialities disappear from the face of the earth the better.'

This kind of thing, this attitude, expressed and unexpressed, towards other peoples was insupportable. Arnold made a deadly comment upon it: 'what I said to myself as I put the newspaper down was this: *Behold England's difficulty in governing Ireland.*' This attitude of the English in their heyday undid a lot of the good work they did in the outside world, the impartial administration of justice they handed down in India, for example: the autobiography of Nehru, himself largely English-educated, shows vividly how the revelation of their attitude turned him into an anti-English, Indian nationalist.

This attitude was even more insupportable within the British Isles, and Arnold rubbed it in that 'in England the Englishman proper is in union of spirit with no one except other Englishmen proper like himself. His Welsh and Irish fellow-citizens are hardly more amalgamated with him now than they were when Wales and Ireland were first conquered, and the true unity of even these small islands has yet to be achieved.' Dr Arnold himself had been one of the worst offenders – a typical example of English insensitiveness, especially considering his marriage. 'When I was young, I was taught to think of Celt as separated by an impassable gulf from Teuton; my father, in particular, was never weary of contrasting them; he insisted much oftener on the separation between us and them than on the separation between us and any other race in the world.' In fact, Dr Arnold never had a good word to say for the Celts; his son was once more in reaction against his father.

Questioned and attacked, Arnold wrote to Fox How to his mother and sister for corroboration: 'I do not think Papa thought of the Saxon and Celt mutually needing to be completed by each other. On the contrary, he was so full of the sense of the Celt's vices, want of steadiness, and want of plain truthfulness, vices to him particularly offensive, that he utterly abhorred him and thought him of no good at all. . . . Can you show me a single line, in all he has written, testifying to his sense of any virtues and graces in the Celt? Ask Tom what he thinks.'

His attention to the possibilities of the subject had been aroused by his meeting with Renan in 1859 and his reading Renan's 'Essay on the Poetry of the Celtic Peoples' with enthusiasm. From this Arnold derived the subject for the last of his narrative poems, 'Saint Brandan', which Froude published in *Fraser's Magazine* next year. Brittany had inspired another poem, 'Stanzas Composed at Carnac', with its evocation of the Celtic scene:

> *Far on its rocky knoll descried*
> *Saint Michael's chapel cuts the sky.*
> *I climbed – beneath me, bright and wide,*
> *Lay the lone coast of Brittany.*
>
> *Bright in the sunset, weird and still,*
> *It lay beside the Atlantic wave,*
> *As if the wizard Merlin's will*
> *Yet charmed it from his forest grave . . .*
>
> *From bush to bush the cuckoo flies,*
> *The orchis red gleams everywhere;*

Gold broom with furze in blossom vies,
The bluebells perfume all the air.

And o'er the glistening lovely land,
Rise up, all round, the Christian spires.
The church of Carnac, by the strand,
Catches the westering sun's last fires.

Arnold had a sense of kinship with Renan, beside the similarity he felt in their vocations, each conceiving of himself as preceptor to his own people. Recommending Renan's book to 'K', he wrote, 'I have long felt that we owed far more, spiritually and artistically, to the Celtic races than the somewhat coarse Germanic intelligence readily perceived, and been increasingly satisfied at our own semi-Celtic origin: which, as I fancy, gives us the power, if we will use it, of comprehending the nature of both races. Renan pushes the glorification of the Celts too far; but there is a great deal of truth in what he says.'

Arnold made this the subject for his next lectures – one might almost say, his next campaign. Though no Celtic scholar, he got up the subject conscientiously, and read what was available to him. He was no Celtic sentimentalist – we have seen that he was opposed to Welsh-speaking in the schools; he wanted the Welsh to learn English and Welsh writers to write in English – to make their work more accessible in the comity of nations. But he was deeply sympathetic, which was more important than sentimentalism; he knew North Wales well and was warm towards the Welsh people, who responded with alacrity – as Celts will, when treated with sympathy. He addressed them a public Letter on their Eisteddfod, in pointed contrast with the tone of *The Times*: 'When I see the enthusiasm these Eisteddfods can awaken in your whole people, and then think of the tastes, the literature, the amusements of our own lower and middle class, I am filled with admiration for you.' On the publication of his lectures he could have had a triumphal tour through Wales, but delined on the ground that he would be accused of 'popularity-seeking'. Too fastidious, as usual: one should never be deterred by what people think, but press on with what one thinks right.

In his public Letter he defined what he meant by 'the "Philistinism" of our middle class. On the side of beauty and taste, vulgarity; on the side of morals and feeling, coarseness; on the side of mind and spirit, unintelligence – this is Philistinism.' Later, Arnold planted some naughty barbs in the hide of very sacred cows to the Victorians: the venerated Luther, who destroyed the unity of Catholic Europe; the Puritan Cromwell, whom Carlyle glorified; the fanatic Bunnion, a cult-figure among Dissenters, to whom Froude devoted a best-selling biography. Freeman and Froude, in other respects so opposed, were both Teutonizers; the irascible Freeman a pillar of the *Saturday Review*, always gunning for Arnold. So – 'we have the Philistine of genius in religion – Luther; the Philistine of genius in politics – Cromwell; the Philistine of genius in literature – Bunnion. All three of them, let us remark, are Germanic, and two of them are English. Mr Freeman must be enchanted.' It was not only the tone that was maddening, but the irony; for Freeman was a liberal High Churchman, who detested all three. It was, indeed, difficult to get back at the elusive Arnold, if only on account of his manner and formal politeness.

He was no ethnologist, for what that was worth, and one does not have to take his generalizations as to national characteristics too heavily, when he put them forward so lightly. On the main issue of the historic make-up of the English people – let alone, more largely, the British – it is extraordinary that he was right as against all the historians of his time. Though he was no historian, common sense told him that there could have been no complete extermination of the original inhabitants when the Saxons conquered them piecemeal, 'and there must be some Celtic vein or other running through us'. The *Saturday Review*, i.e. Professor Freeman, thought not. Arnold continued to laugh at him, and the 'popular opinion' held that all the Britons 'were destroyed or expelled'. With imagination and perception he argued, 'attached to the soil, they will have shared in that emancipation which during the course of the Middle Ages gradually restored to political life the mass of the population in the countries of Western Europe; recovering by slow degrees their rights without resuming their name, and rising gradually with the rise of industry, they will have got spread through all ranks of society.'

The modern historian can say that this is a just, as well as imaginative, perception of the process of emergence of submerged peoples. One does not need to cite famous names of Celts making their contribution to the cultural amalgam, from Asser to Kipling; one can confine oneself to Arnold's reference to 'political life', and observe the emergence of the submerged in conspicuous figures of this century. Take the Celtic element among Prime Ministers alone: Lloyd George, MacDonald, Macmillan; Campbell-Bannerman was, after all, a Campbell, Baldwin on his mother's side a Macdonald. (Lloyd George said of him, 'understand Baldwin? Of course, you can't: he is one of us.')

Arnold confessed to 'a great *penchant* for the Celtic races, their melancholy and unprogressiveness'. He did not like the Germans – what person of taste or culture, except in music, could? On his educational mission of 1865, he found that 'the Germans, with their hideousness and their commonness, are no relief to one's spirit, but rather depress it. Never surely was there seen a people of so many millions so unattractive. . . . The whole middle class hates refinement and disbelieves in it; this makes North Germany, where the middle class has it – socially though not governmentally – all its own way, so intensely unattractive and disagreeable. . . . They all dislike England, though with their tongue perhaps more than their hearts.' This was already thus early, in 1865: their corrosive envy was to gather strength more and more, until it led to its upshot in 1914 and 1939, the ultimate catastrophe of 1945.

What makes this important is that Arnold was going against the mainstream, the whole tide, of contemporary society and thought, with its admiration for everything German. Here one must discriminate: the achievements of German music and science were pre-eminent, in scholarship excellent, particularly in giving new impulses; in philosophy, at best dubious, at the worst disastrous; in politics and power, ruinous, putting the clock back in Europe for over a century. Arnold's own attitude was ambivalent: he exaggerated the importance of German literature, which was not to be compared with French or English, Italian or Spanish; but he depreciated the language, admirable as it is for poetry and poetic prose, as with Hölderlin or Nietzsche, much inferior to French as a medium of rational communication.

At the least we must subscribe to Arnold's option for variety and diversity, though he had difficulty in distinguishing Celtic characteristics: he wrote to his mother, 'when one has to treat a subtle matter such as I have been treating now, the marks of a Celtic leaven subsisting in the English spirit and its productions, it is very difficult to satisfy oneself.' It is still more difficult today: the spurious racialist nonsense fostered by the Germans, at its apogee under Hitler, has disinclined people from distinguishing sense in the matter. Though impossible perhaps to define, we can all recognize the fact of group, national or racial characteristics: we can tell a Chinese from an Indian, a Frenchman from a German or Russian, an Englishman from a Welshman or Irishman.

Arnold considered that Celts were 'sentimental – *always ready to react against the despotism of fact*': he was thinking of the Irish, though the author of the phrase was thinking of the Bretons. 'An organisation quick to feel impressions, and feel them very strongly; a lively personality, therefore, keenly sensitive to joy and sorrow; this is the main point.' He added other traits – an undertone of melancholy beneath the mercurial surface, a nature 'sociable, hospitable, eloquent, figuring away brilliantly' – one thinks of Aneurin Bevan or Dylan Thomas. One could improve on Arnold, adding such touches as the acute personalism, the enlarged ego, of Celts, the touchiness and pernicketiness – where the English are more stolid, easier to get on with, perhaps *too* easy-going.

It is not our business to follow Arnold's excursus into Celtic literature, but to indicate something of the effect he had. His name and advocacy helped to put Celtic concerns and studies on the map; there was a great expansion of Celtic scholarship in Western Europe in the later nineteenth century. It had consequences beyond the field of scholarship, in literature, for example, and in the rise of political nationalism. The English could never regard themselves as simply Anglo-Saxons again: it was too obvious that they were of mixed stocks, it would be more comprehensive to describe them as Anglo-Celtic. Arnold ended his lectures with a plea for the foundation of a chair of Celtic at Oxford, and 'to send through the gentle ministration of science, a message of peace to Ireland'. The chair was duly founded, and has played a part in the encouragement of Celtic scholarship. But history has shown that the only message that Ireland would ultimately entertain from the English was that they should get out.

Arnold sent his lectures to Renan when they were published, since he owed a good deal to the leading Breton of the time – and was duly attacked as too pro-French: which he was. Arnold always felt at home in France. Clough's health was now failing; Arnold suggested, 'why not try Brittany? easy of access, cheap, a climate that would suit you (as cold as England) and deeply interesting.' Clough's family came from North Wales, where Arnold felt much at home. 'The charm of Wales is the extent of the country . . . and then the new race, language and literature give it a charm and novelty which the Lake country can never have. Wales is as full of traditions and associations as Cumberland and Westmorland are devoid of them.' This was very disloyal to the Doctor, who had fixed the Arnolds fatally at Fox How. Matt would have liked a farm among the Welsh mountains; from North Wales he writes, in the summer of 1864, 'the poetry of the Celtic race and its names of places quite overpowers me.' In the Lectures he cites such names as Velindra, Tintagel, Caernarvon, 'with their penetrating, lofty beauty', as against homely Weathersfield, Thaxted, Shalford, smacking of the soil. 'And it will be long before Tom forgets the line,

Hear from thy grave, great Taliessin, hear! –

from Gray's Bard, of which I gave him the benefit some hundred times a day on our excursions.'

Earlier Arnold had written to Clough, 'to be among Tals and Pens and Llans makes my thoughts turn to you at once. . . . You should have been with me tonight to see the sunset of our first fine day over the great Caernarvonshire promontory. What an outline is

that! The most accurate lurid Mediterranean thing in these islands.'
Clough died in the Mediterranean, his remarkable promise unful-
filled, at Florence in November 1861. Arnold confided to his mother,
'that is a loss which I shall feel more and more as time goes on, for
he is one of the few people who ever made a deep impression upon
me.' To Clough's widow he wrote, 'our friendship was more important to me than it was to him, and no one will ever again be to me
what he was.' He never defined what moved him so much in Clough,
when intellectually they differed so markedly. Can it have been that,
unconscious to both, they were fellow-Celts? That the feeling
reached to the root of his being – otherwise a rather cool, defeated
nature – is clear from the fact that the poem he wrote in Clough's
memory, 'Thyrsis', is one of his most inspired. Mrs Clough sent him
some of Clough's last lines: 'I shall take them with me to Oxford,
where I shall go alone after Easter [1862]; and there, among the
Cumnor hills where we have so often rambled, I shall be able to
think him over as I could wish.'

The result was a poem which is as capable today – a hundred years
after – as then, of affecting one to tears, such is the intensity of the
evocation of those loved scenes.

> *I know these slopes: who knows them if not I? –*
> *But many a dingle on the loved hillside,*
> *With thorns once studded, old, white blossomed trees,*
> *Where thick the cowslips grew and, far descried,*
> *High towered the spikes of purple orchises,*
> *Hath since our day put by*
> *The coronals of that forgotten time.*
> *Down each green bank hath gone the ploughboy's team,*
> *And only in the hidden brookside gleam*
> *Primroses, orphans of the flowery prime.*
>
> *Where is the girl who, by the boatman's door,*
> *Above the locks, above the boating throng,*
> *Unmoored our skiff when, through the Wytham flats,*
> *Red loosestrife and blond meadowsweet among,*
> *And darting swallows, and light water-gnats,*

We tracked the shy Thames shore?
Where are the mowers who, as the tiny swell
Of our boat passing heaved the river-grass,
Stood with suspended scythe to see us pass? –
They all are gone, and thou art gone as well.

In prefacing his *Essays in Criticism*, which contained some of his Lectures, Arnold paid a celebrated prose-tribute to Oxford, launching some of the phrases for which he was now known, several of which have remained with us: that city, 'whispering from her towers the last enchantments of the Middle Age', 'home of lost causes, and forsaken beliefs, and unpopular names [Newman's and his own], and impossible loyalties!' Now, in 1867, to celebrate the term of his Professorship, he brought out a volume of *New Poems*, his last, which contained, besides 'Saint Brandan' and the 'Stanzas Composed at Carnac', 'Thyrsis', the most marvellous evocation of Oxford ever written.

CHAPTER 6

Prophet of Secondary Education

ARNOLD'S PROFESSIONAL ROUTINE was concerned with primary education, 'the dance of death in the elementary school'. We know what a
weariness of the flesh this was to the soul of a poet, an addict of
mountains and essentially a countryman. In the autumn of 1858, 'I
have not yet got over the profound disgust which the first loss of the
country creates in me at my return to London, and with the prospect
of tramping on stone pavements for nine months to come.' From
Marble Arch to Belgravia he found impenetrable fog. At the end of
January 1859, 'I have written so little of late because I am over-
whelmed with grammar papers to be looked over, and – not choos-
ing, as I grow older and my time shortens, to give up my own work
entirely for any routine business – I have a hard time of it just at
present. When I have finished these papers I have a General Report
and a Training School Report to get out of hand, the inspection of
schools going on alongside of this all the while.'

It may be imagined with what relief he welcomed the invitation
to go abroad for five months on a mission to report on higher
education in schools – 'free from routine work, of which I sometimes
get very sick, and to be dealing with its history and principles. Then
foreign life is still to me perfectly delightful, and *liberating* in the
highest degree . . . when I think of the borders of the lake of Geneva
in May, and the narcissuses and the lilies, I can hardly sit still.'

The mission was to have more important consequences than
liberating Matthew Arnold. It resulted in a book, *A French Eton*,
always a favourite with him, which alerted public opinion to the
backwardness and confusion of secondary education, compared with
the Continent. The convenient phrase 'secondary' education was

Arnold's, imported from France. The mission had the effect of directing his mind henceforward, more and more, to the necessity of improving the chaotic provision for middle-class education in Public Schools, old and new, grammar schools, private schools, commercial and industrial schools, sectarian academies, what not. As Arnold said, popular education – lower-class education – was now fairly launched and safe: the impulse would carry on. There remained the vast area between the elementary schools and the universities and colleges, which was quite unco-ordinated, ill provided and without direction or supervision.

What Arnold discerned was that, altogether, the proportion of children receiving some sort of secondary education in England was only one-half that in France, under the state direction of the Second Empire. And this at a time when the prosperity of the English middle classes was bounding as never before. The reason for this state of affairs, and the great disparities and defects within such secondary education as existed, was much the same as that which had impeded the proper development of elementary education – the nation-wide resistance to the intervention of the state. This was at its most intense with the Nonconformists – and they had immensely increased their political and social power with the expansion of the Victorian middle class, in industry and trade.

From now on Arnold found a new field of activity, rather different in character: on top of his continuing drudgery as elementary-school inspector, he became the leading propagandist for a proper system of secondary education for the nation. His daily routine was not with these schools. He was sent abroad again by the Commission of 1865 for a wider Report on Schools and Universities in France and Germany. This, too, was published and had much influence with the Commission. His educational writings henceforth are mainly concerned with this subject, articles, reports, letters, books; his last article appeared in the year of his retirement, only two years before his death. It was here that he exerted his grandest influence, and built up a following that carried his ideas into action. A Permanent Secretary of the Education Department was a disciple; so, too, were such men as Morrell, and the dynamic pair Morant and Michael

Sadler. When the national system of secondary education was at last constructed with the Act of 1902, it was largely in accordance with Arnold's ideas. With it, his impact upon society, unrealized except by 'educationists' – again another concept of his – was vastly greater than his more publicized father's.

We perceive that the French influence upon Arnold was no less in this field than in the literary sphere. His official mission opened all doors to him, not only writers and government officials, but inaccessible reactionary archbishops and reclusive spirits such as the eminent Père Lacordaire. He spent one or two evenings with Sainte-Beuve, whose conversation he 'would not have missed for all the world'; he met Mérimée and Renan, while Villemain introduced him as *un Anglais qui nous juge parfaitement*. Arnold's new departure in political pamphleteering, *England and the Italian Question*, with its sympathetic presentation of the case for the unification of Italy, made him talked about; for it was while he was in Paris that Napoleon III embarked on the brief war with Austria that liberated Italy. Arnold's pamphlet, much approved in Paris, was sent on to Cavour. No doubt this played its part in the King of Italy sending his younger son, the Duke of Genoa, to learn English in Arnold's family later.

He has his own perceptive comments on the Second Empire. He thought that the Emperor was too deferential to the Ultramontane views of the Church, and hoped that he would not withdraw until Venice was liberated as well as Lombardy. He observed the lasting effect of the Revolution on French society: 'the profoundly democratic spirit which exists among the lower orders, even among the Breton peasants. Not a spirit which will necessarily be turbulent, but a spirit which has irrevocably broken with the past, and which makes the revival of an aristocratic society impossible. . . . The Revolution has cleared out the feudal ages from the minds of the country people to an extent incredible with us.'

Arrived in Alsace he has a very telling comment: 'You know the people here are among the Frenchest of the French, in spite of their German race and language. It strikes one as something unnatural to see this German town and German-speaking people all mad for joy

at a victory gained by the French over the Germans [i.e. Solferino].
. . . The Rhine provinces in 1815, after having belonged to France
for only ten years, objected exceedingly to being given back to
Germany.' What a tribute this was to something inherently attractive in French civilization! He did not, at this point, draw the contrast
with the failure of the English to attract the Irish into their orbit.

Dr Arnold's friend, the Protestant historian Guizot, had founded
the national system of primary education in France with his Act of
1833. His successors had developed a comparable system of secondary
education, with a Minister of Public Instruction at the head of the
whole vast, but rationally co-ordinated, organization. This was what
Arnold wanted to see achieved in England. The system was universal,
unimpeded by the sectarian obstruction raised by Nonconformists;
for, in France, the state gave its support to denominational schools,
leaving religion to the denominations (in practice, mainly the
Catholic Church), with a large inspectorate of five hundred to
supervise the education. The system was a state system, and thus
enjoyed uniformity; every department had its central *lycée*, and
Arnold said that when you had seen one you had seen all.

A French Eton or Middle-Class Education and the State begins by
puncturing the humbug of *The Times* about 'the real ruler of our
country being "The People" – although this potentate does not
absolutely transact his own business, but delegates that function to the
class which Eton educates.' He continues by poking fun at regarding
the operation of supply and demand as sufficient to provide a nation's
education: 'The mass of mankind do not so well know what dis-
tinguishes good teaching and training from bad; they do not here
know what they ought to demand, and therefore the demand cannot
be relied on to give us the right supply.' *The Times* talks beautifully
of 'the fetters of endowment and the interference of the executive' –
'happy country! happy middle classes! Well may *The Times* con-
gratulate them with such fervency. . . . We trusted to [demand and
supply] to give us fit elementary schools till its impotence became
conspicuous; we have thrown it aside, and called upon state-aid to
give us elementary schools more like what they should be.' . . . Now,

'to see secondary instruction treated as a matter of national concern, to see any serious attempt to make it both commensurate with the numbers needing it and of good quality, we must cross the Channel.'

Irritating as this was to the self-complacency of the Victorian English, Arnold brought it home to them in the terms they best understood – their pockets: 'Why cannot we have throughout England – as the French have throughout France, as the Germans have throughout Germany, as the Swiss have throughout Switzerland, as the Dutch have throughout Holland – schools where the children of our middle and professional classes may obtain, at the rate of from £20 to £50 a year, if they are boarders, or from £5 to £15 a year if they are day-scholars, an education of as good quality, with as good guarantees, social character and advantages for a future career in the world as the education which French children of the corresponding class can obtain?' The English reply that they have the incomparable Eton and Harrow. No doubt, 'the English Public School produces the finest boys in the world . . . but Eton and Harrow cannot produce him for much less than £200 a year.' They are evidently for the upper classes. Even 'Winchester and Rugby produce him at about £120 a year.' Matt adds disloyally that the meals at the French *lycée* 'though plain, are good, and they are set out with a propriety and a regard for appearances which, when I was a boy, graced no school-dinners that ever I saw.' He spoke up, too, for the neatness of the meals in the Normal Schools for elementary teachers: 'With us it is always the individual that is filled, and the public that is sent empty away.'

We must not go into the detailed information which Arnold reported for the benefit of the English public, but note the general characteristics and principles which might with advantage be applied at home. The chief town of each department had its *lycée*, and its considerable towns their communal colleges; the teachers supplied by the Normal School, 'the unique and best part of French secondary instruction'. All this had been achieved by the energy and direction of the state. ' "But the state", says *The Times*, "can hardly aid education without cramping and warping its growth, and mischievously interfering with the laws of natural development." '

Arnold replied that 'for public establishments modern societies have to betake themselves to the state; that is, *to themselves in their collective and corporate character.*' In the circumstances of nineteenth-century Europe, 'the education of each class in society has, or ought to have, its ideal, determined by the wants of that class, and by its destination.' He could imagine a society so uniform that one education would do for all its members, but no such society existed in fact. (It is ironical today, when English society, under the influence of its illusory liberalism, is levelling education downwards, that Communist Russia, without illusions about human nature in general, is establishing select schools after the older English type – essential to effective leadership in a society.)

Arnold paid tribute to the profound political sense of the old aristocracy in following its instinct for the preservation of its own order: in this, 'they signally display their best virtues, moderation, prudence, sagacity; they prevent fruitful occasions of envy, dissension, and strife.' (We may observe that they lost their touch after the holocaust of the first German war.) Arnold thought it natural that the aristocracy should be jealous of state interference with their privileges, while 'the working classes have no antipathy to state action. . . . It is the middle class that has been this action's great enemy. The stronghold of Nonconformity then [in the seventeenth century] as now, was in the middle class; in its struggle to repel the conformity forced upon it, the middle class underwent great suffering and injustice; and it has never forgotten them.'

This was a Victorian view, much too favourable to the Puritans who, intolerantly and intolerably, aimed at forcing their narrow views on others: in the course of their destructive attempt they got much less than they asked for, and suffered a great deal less than they deserved, considering what they destroyed. However, though Arnold was a middle-class man himself and quite fair enough to the Nonconformists, we see what his targets had to be, if the country was to realize a system of secondary education, in which it was decades behind France and Germany.

Of the aristocracy he thought 'the culture of this class is not what it used to be.' There is something in this when one compares the stan-

dard of taste of the eighteenth-century aristocracy with the Victorian;
or if one considers the culture of such men as Pitt and Fox, Canning
and Melbourne. Arnold had the justice to admit that 'it is the middle
class which has real mental ardour, real curiosity; it is the middle
class which is the great reader' – and called forth the prolific literature
of the age, of which he himself had too low, too supercilious an
opinion. From the point of view of education, however, he could
not be on stronger ground: if the working classes were to receive an
education, the middle classes needed education to perform the task.

He perceived that they were divided. The professional middle class
were educated along with the upper class and shared its standards.
The commercial and industrial middle class had lower standards,
and approximated to the lower orders in their lack of cultivation.
Arnold's ideal was to bring them together, achieve more harmony,
and that could only be by uniform state-action.

The charming part of *A French Eton* is Arnold's account of his visit
to Lacordaire's famous private school at Sorrèze, near Toulouse.
Arnold felt a real kinship with this elect spirit, once a preacher whose
audience filled Notre Dame to hear him, now a secluded Dominican
dedicated to his school. (Today there are schools named after him all
over France.) Arnold had heard from Lacordaire's pupils how much
he admired Oxford – he probably felt a similarity between the
Oxford Movement's revival of life in the English Church and the
movement in France begun by Lamennais and himself. Arnold
attended the service in chapel and was much impressed by it.

For once he allowed himself the luxury of an emotional peroration,
addressed to the working classes: 'Children of the future, whose day
has not yet dawned, you, when that day arrives, will hardly believe
what obstructions were long suffered to prevent its coming! You,
who, with all your faults, have neither the aridity of aristocracies, nor
the narrow-mindedness of middle classes, you, whose power of
simple enthusiasm is your great gift, will not comprehend how
progress towards man's best perfection should have been reluctantly
undertaken; how it should have been for years and years retarded. . . .
You will know nothing of the doubts, the fears, the prejudices they
[its friends] had to dispel; nothing of the outcry they had to en-

counter. . . . But you, in your turn, with difficulties of your own, will then be mounting some new step in the arduous ladder whereby man climbs towards his perfection. . . .' And so on.

A working-class man myself, I acknowledge gratefully all that we owe to Arnold and his disciples in prising open the opportunities for our education – such a contrast with the scant chances our parents had! In my time I was able to witness in remote Cornwall the inspiration the next generation of these disciples had received, and the noble idealism with which they carried out the nation-wide impulse given by the Act of 1902. Such a man as Quiller-Couch was a Cliftonian – and Clifton was directly inspired by the Rugby of Dr Arnold, as others of the new Public Schools were, like Marlborough and Uppingham.

At the same time I am bound to own that Matthew Arnold's idealized picture of the working class was a middle-class one – I do not share it, any more than Carlyle, who had been a poor peasant, shared W. E. Forster's middle-class view of the poor. Carlyle shocked the highminded Forster by his coarse realism, Forster's admiration for Carlyle wilted in consequence; Matthew Arnold simply came to regard him as 'a moral desperado'. The labours of these devoted middle-class idealists, Arnold and Forster, gave the working class their just opportunity to be educated. How far its members make the most of the opportunities so hardly won must now rest with themselves – Arnold and his disciples would be sickened by the disappointment of many of their hopes. Even before the end of his course Arnold glimpsed that the masses were hardly capable of education in any significant sense of the word – only the elect are: he saw that what it amounted to, generally speaking, was educating them to read the newspapers. In our time, it means a preference for not even reading, but passively imbibing television.

In 1865 Arnold was given an opportunity for yet wider travel on the Continent – France, Italy, Germany – to report this time on Higher Schools and Universities. Reports resulted from his tour which he turned into books: *Schools and Universities on the Continent*, in 1868, soon went out of print. Arnold republished part of this, with a new long polemical Preface, as *Higher Schools and Universities in Germany*, in 1874; while the French section was republished with *A French Eton* after his death. These works were witnesses to his growing influence over the whole sphere of higher education.

The realization of this, with the added interest of his Continental experience, must have had its effect in reconciling him to the drudging side of his work. Not only this – it engaged his mind to such an extent that he actually says, in the 1870s, 'the times are wonderful': he could see the progress being made and this gave him hope – on the public side of his life; no more on the inner than before. This is what we mean by saying that his father eventually won in him.

Earlier he had tried to free himself: he even thought of going out to Mauritius as Secretary of the colony, but his good angel of counsel, Lingen, dissuaded him. He had fancied a political career, but he had no money; his brother-in-law Forster had and could afford it – a Quaker, he thought of it as public service. To some considerable extent Arnold could look to Forster to carry out his educational ideas in Parliament; when Forster became Chief Secretary for Ireland, Arnold's interest in Ireland quickened and he devoted several later essays to the Irish question – a sympathetic, independent, non-party view, as always. Arnold was thought of for the educational Commission, and possibly for its Secretary. In 1867 he applied for the Librarianship of the House of Commons – in vain. He said that he could never expect any promotion or government appointment at Gladstone's hands. And, indeed, he never was awarded anything for his lifetime of public service, except a DCL at Oxford from Lord Salisbury.

In 1870 he was raised to the new rank of Senior Inspector; he was shackled to the cause of Education. We may see a providence, or at least a propriety, in that; for here he had an historic contribution to make – and made it.

He was well pleased with his assignment in 1865, six months leave of absence: 'the Report I must write while going on with my schools as usual. I did *not* want to be a Commissioner, I did *not* want to be Secretary, but I *did* want to go abroad, and to Germany as well as France. . . . When I see the chestnut leaves coming out in the Tuileries gardens under the April weather, I shall again feel the charm and stir of travel again, as I did when I was young.'

Stopping at the Hôtel Meurice in the Rue de Rivoli, he did not much care for the new look that Haussmann had given Paris, with his wide boulevards. 'They make Paris, which used to be the most historic place in the world, one monotonous handsomer Belgravia.' However, he was made much of in Paris, as usual, and was introduced to Byron's mistress, the Guiccioli, who had survived to this date. (This enables one to appreciate how comparatively close Arnold was to Byron, Shelley and Keats – only one generation intervened: they all might have lived to meet him.) He renewed his acquaintance with the French theatre, which 'both for acting and for a study of the language, is just what the English theatre is not, where the acting is detestable, and the mode of speaking is just what one ought *not* to adopt.' Sainte-Beuve took him to the Princess Mathilde's salon, in her magnificent mansion, formerly Queen Christina's, where were all the literary and official notabilities, including Prince Napoleon, the independent-minded 'Plon-Plon' – much more of a Bonaparte than the Emperor. The Papal Nuncio provided Arnold with letters which enabled him to see the Jesuit schools. An American was able to inform him that his *Essays in Criticism* was already republished in America, 'and that I shall get something for them; but we shall see.' (In the absence of copyright protection many English authors received nothing from America for their work.)

This time his tour included Italy, and he had the historic chance of witnessing 'a nation of 22 million changing its capital and transforming its public business', from Turin to Florence, a halt on the way to Rome in a few years time. He was not much impressed by the new kingdom, a rather ramshackle affair, and the Church was doing all it could to oppose and obstruct: 'The government is omnipotent here at this moment, and the Ministers are the only people in the country who really work. They do. They have to make the nation, and I hope in time it may be done.' As for the schools, the buildings were fine, because the governments had handed over the convents it had suppressed; but 'I am tempted to take the professors I see in the schools by the collar, and hold them down to their work for five or six hours a day – so angry do I get at their shirking and inefficiency.' This kind of thing went all through the newly unified country; he considered the Piedmontese the only virile element in it.

'I have got to speak the language, for practical purposes, tolerably; but I generally find French does.' He spoke French, German, and Italian; in addition to the classical languages, he later learned some Hebrew. How many Victorians had such breadth of culture? Rather un-English, he was a good European.

Going on to Germany, he missed the Italian charm: 'I am left alone with this, the most *bourgeois* of nations . . . they have all the merits and defects which this definition implies. . . . Their schools are excellent.' In Berlin he found 'Papa's name and work are very well known here. Berlin is a fine city, but its sole interest for me comes from Frederick the Great, one of the half dozen really great moderns.' Here was another Victorian cult-figure – it does not appear that the Victorians appreciated *all* that was to be known about Frederick the Great, any more than about their venerated Vaughan, Head-master of Harrow. Very interestingly, Arnold saw through the ineffectiveness of German Liberals: 'this Bismarck knows, and it is the secret of the contempt with which he treats the Liberals.'

When Arnold came to write his Report, however, he did justice to the wisdom of Bismarck's policy in allowing the Catholics to run their own schools (the unwisdom of the *Kulturkampf* came later). In his polemical Preface to the work when published as a book, Arnold contrasted this with the narrowness of the Nonconformists at home in objecting to Catholic education in Ireland – and there is a thorough-going attack on the dreadful Miall. Arnold was wholly sympathetic to the Catholics running their own university. He says summarily, 'in short, Roman Catholicism is not a *lie*; it is, like Protestantism itself, an essay in religion, an approximation.' This was calculated to give pleasure to neither side, for each claimed the possession of absolute truth, of course. No doubt the effect was calculated: Arnold intended to put both in their place and expose their mutually ex-clusive claims. Today, with ecumenism, Arnold has won; here, too, we see how long-sighted a prophet he was.

Arnold's options were not the simple Protestant options of the

Victorians with their favourite heroes of the Reformation. He preferred the Renaissance: 'in England our best spirits – Shakespeare, Bacon, Spenser – were men of the Renaissance, and our Reformers were men of the second order.' Not a historian, he could hardly be expected to know that there was a Renaissance strain carried over into Protestantism (Spenser exemplified it); that there were Protestant humanists, like Melancthon, truly ecumenical in spirit, whose Erasmian sympathies were much in line with the English Church. Arnold saw how much wiser the Church had been to stand by catholicity and historic tradition than to attach itself to narrow Protestant doctrine. (Evidently something of Newman's sermons in St Mary's had percolated after all.)

Arnold much approved the systematic teaching of their own language in French schools, and disapproved of the neglect of English in English schools. He was modern-minded enough to give his approval to the study of English literature – a new thought then – in universities. He went on to bring home the objective of all his preaching: 'the ideal of a general, liberal training is, to carry us to a knowledge of ourselves and the world.' And, once more: 'our dislike of authority and our disbelief in science have combined to make us leave our school system, like so many other branches of our civil organisation, to take care of itself as best it could.' Further, 'if public schools are a necessity, then an Education Minister is a necessity.'

Critics of Arnold, like *The Times*, did not fail to point out that appointments under such a national system as prevailed in France and Germany would be influenced by political considerations. This must be admitted – and to that extent there was greater freedom in England. At the same time the tacit assumptions of English society were so powerful that no real opponent of the system was likely to gain promotion; and any outsider who has watched the operation of the Old School Tie bond in the upper ranges of English society even in my time – in literary life no less than educational (Etonians back each other in the literary journals or the Sunday newspapers, Wykehamists in Oxford colleges) – knows that no word need be *said*.

In any case, the urgent point of Arnold's Report remains: 'England, with her wealth and importance has barely one-half the proportion

of her population coming – even nominally – under superior instruction, that Prussia and France have.' And even Oxford and
Cambridge, Arnold considered as merely *hauts lycées*. This was in
keeping with the views of Liberal reformers at Oxford, like Jowett
and Pattison – but that was not Arnold's field. He was naturally
sympathetic to the objectives of the new university colleges coming
into being. In London he wished to see University College and King's
College co-ordinated to make a proper university, with full 'faculties
formed in connexion with it, in order to give some public voice and
place to superior instruction in the richest capital in the world.
London would then really have, what it has not at present, a university.'

He was keenly pleased by the creation of new university colleges
at Liverpool and Manchester, before he had run his course, and
suggested that the state might add dignity to these institutions by
assigning Regius professorships to them. Again, the early years of
this century saw a wonderful enthusiasm inspire the beginnings of
the young civic universities, notably at Liverpool and Manchester,
Leeds and Sheffield – and some of the exemplars of this idealistic
spirit, such men as Sadler, Moberly, H. A. L. Fisher, recognizably
derived inspiration from Arnold.

In 1867 he did receive a public tribute from a quarter he respected,
all the more agreeable because it took him by surprise. It was at the
farewell banquet for Dickens, off to America. Lord Lytton, who was
in the chair, turned aside to pay a warm tribute to Arnold, who was
present to honour Dickens. Arnold was much touched by the un-
wontedness of it, and on such an occasion. He wrote to thank Lytton:
'I have had very little success with the general public, and I sincerely
think that it is a fault in an author not to succeed with his general
public, and that the great authors are those who do succeed with it.'
We see that Arnold mixed with his modesty a certain resentment, or
at least *ressentiment* – he knew his own value well enough. This led
to a friendship between the poet–school inspector and the rich,
romantic Earl, who was also a bestseller. Arnold recognized 'a
certain European tone of reflection and sentiment in your writings,
which impressed me and suited me from the first times when I began

to read at all'. His reservations as to the mingled grandeur and gim-crackery of Knebworth, characteristic of its eminent owner, he confined to his family.

In 1870 Forster carried through his historic Education Act, which at last gave the working classes a nation-wide system of primary education. A new Liberal government provided the impetus, the only chance of an Education Bill for years: Forster seized it with both hands, with the utter devotion, public spirit and sense of justice of the Quaker he was. Though it was his own handiwork and he deserves all the credit, we may observe how much it is in agreement with the principles Arnold had been urging for years: he, his sister 'K' (Forster's wife), and Forster made an effective trio, at one with each other.

The main difficulty was the strategic one of how to steer it through the conflict, and the pressures, of the sects. On one wing were the political Nonconformists, led by Miall, whose main concern was that the Church should not gain any advantage – these were the most powerful opponents. They themselves were divided: Baines led a more moderate group, which ultimately accepted the Bill, leaving Miall, defeated, mad for Disestablishment of the Church. On the other wing were the Secularist Radicals, inspired by the advanced ideas of Mill and Morley, who were opposed to any religious teaching in the schools.

The just-minded Quaker chose the middle of the road, the only course that represented something like a consensus of opinion, at any rate the majority. The largest number of voluntary schools were Church schools. Forster retained them within the new national system, supplementing them where they did not exist with new schools. On the ferocious question of religious teaching, he decided in favour of Bible reading and instruction by the teachers. This was the best practical solution for the time; it did no harm – the Bible was above question – and it provided that 'morality touched with emotion' which Arnold considered the best prescription for people in general. It was all very well for a hermit-philosopher like F. H. Bradley to attack Arnold's phrase as meaningless, or tautologous, or logically indefensible, but it answered the practical need.

Forster wrote to Kingsley that, while the sects quarrelled, their 'children are growing up savages, while *they* are trying to prevent one another from helping them'. Dr Hook, the admirable vicar of Leeds, recognized the religious controversy for what it was, 'a political squabble'; we may add that it was also a nonsense squabble – a great deal of human fuss and fume is over nonsense. Actually, the Church, as the largest and most nearly national body, came well out of it – it is said that Arnold's sister, with the sympathies of the family, had a considerable influence with her husband in that direction.

The country in general responded with public spirit to the historic measure. School Boards were formed all over the country, on which the various interests were represented, and local people of initiative and ability readily served. The results speak for themselves. Before 1870 some 8,000 schools were inspected, with an average attendance of just over 1 million; 28,000 elementary teachers. By 1886, 19,000 schools were inspected; average attendance, $3\frac{1}{2}$ million; 87,000 teachers; and there were some 2,225 School Boards. Arnold wanted to see the management of the schools transferred to properly constituted local authorities: he did not fancy either squire or clergyman being able to say, proprietorially, '*my* school'. He argued in favour of county committees. This had to wait till 1888, the year of his death, when the setting up of County Councils provided the focus for the development of the LEAs, the Local Education Authorities, which did an historic job in the development of both primary and secondary education all over the country, up to the social revolution of our time.

This, which may be regarded as the classic period in the evolution of the nation's education, was inspired by the ideas of Arnold more than anyone else. Hence their excellence: the ideal of comprehensiveness, based fundamentally on that of classical humanism coming down from the Renaissance; considerable sympathy with the development and teaching of modern science (Arnold was a friend of Huxley, and the families, as we have seen, were drawn together by marriage); an undoctrinal, non-sectarian religious teaching, upholding good standards, 'morality touched by emotion', in practice. The principles exemplified by the most lofty poet of the age, who stood for quality and as much equality as was compatible with it, the best standards in literature, reading and teaching, could hardly have been bettered. The nation had reason to be proud that its educational system, in the classic modern period, was inspired from such a source.

It may well be doubted whether the erosion of quality in the interests of equality, the sacrifice of educational standards in pursuit of social objectives, the levelling downwards of a mass-civilization, will achieve such results in excellence and cultural creativeness as the epoch which preceded it: Arnold's age.

Now for middle-class education, and its heterogeneous, unco-ordinated schools ranging all the way from Eton to Mr Creakle's Academy in *David Copperfield*: 'Mr Creakle's school at Blackheath is the type of our ordinary middle class schools, and our middle class is satisfied that it should be so.' Arnold was very hard on the Victorian middle class: he described it as 'among the worst educated in the world'. It is hardly surprising that he was so much attacked, when he minced no words in describing the middle classes, prospering, in-creasingly well off, and well satisfied with themselves. Think of 'their way of life, their habits, their manners, the very tones of their voice; look at them attentively; observe the literature they read, the things which give them pleasure, the words which come out of their mouths, the thoughts that make the furniture of their minds: would any amount of wealth be worth having with the condition that one was to become like these people?'

Could supercilious disapproval go further? It is like the contempt for everything *bourgeois* that inspired Flaubert throughout life.

It is unlikely that the French middle class were much better, though Arnold, with his respect for everything French, thought so. And he had an important point to urge. In France there was not the marked division between the professional and the commercial classes: they shared a common culture and were more homogeneous because they had the same education. Arnold wished to see what was, after all, his own middle class rendered more homogeneous by a properly inte-grated system of secondary education. He thought, among other things, that it would reduce its inferiority-complex towards the upper classes.

More important was the fact that power was coming into the hands of the middle class; the past lay with the aristocracy, the distant future with the working class. If these last were to be educated then the middle class must be properly educated in order to civilize the masses. And 'the master-thought by which my politics are governed is this – the thought of the bad civilization of the English middle class.' (This was in 1879.) There was 'the dismal and illiberal life on which I have so often touched . . . business, chapels, tea-meetings, and addresses from Mr Murphy and the Rev. W. Cattle.' I do not know who these paragons were, but they were eclipsed by the veneration with which the celebrated Spurgeon was regarded, and the vast City Temple which was built to hold the following that came to hear him. And the news-value he had! the money he made! 'Seriousness, few amusements, religion and work were the hallmarks of the middle class in the new towns, where all that was not labour was middle class', so concludes the economic historian, Clapham, in corroboration of Arnold.

After the achievement of Forster's Education Act we find Arnold broadening the front of his campaign not only to concern himself with secondary education and the middle classes but with the problems of Victorian society in general: the claims of social equality as against its 'religion of inequality', its literary and religious culture, and so into specific political issues such as Ireland and the future of British Liberalism. Not that he neglected his elementary-school work, now that the battle there was won. We find him moving into new ground with his insistence upon the provision of better textbooks and the relegation of inferior trash which he made fun of. He urged good selections from the poets, and himself set a model with a volume giving the best of Wordsworth: in itself a distinguished little book, it achieved a circulation that was a surprise to him, inured to the small sales of his own works.

His volume of 1879, *Mixed Essays*, displays this broader front; that entitled, *Porro Unum est Necessarium* – the one thing needful – devoted to middle-class education, sums up his position on the subject and aroused wider attention than before. He complained that his

Reports and books of 1859 and 1864 had had as yet no effect – the middle class had been content to go on in the same old way, in spite of the evident disadvantages to themselves. He pointed out that they supported the cost of elementary education for the working class; at the same time the upper classes had annexed to themselves a sizeable proportion of the endowments originally intended for the middle class. It is odd that they should not have resented this; but a number of the Public Schools had been transformed from grammar schools founded for the people of their localities – Harrow, Rugby, Shrewsbury, Repton, Blundell's, to instance only a few.

One observes how much Arnold's educational and social criticism is dominated by the concept of Class – no one thought so significantly in these terms, except Marx, who was rather outside Arnold's ken. It may be that his social awareness was sharpened by the fact that he was himself a middle-class man educated in accordance with aristocratic standards – a situation prevailing in England unlike that in France, where a homogeneous middle class, more uniformly educated, dominated the nation. 'In England the government is composed of a string of aristocratical personages, with one or two men from the professional class who are engaged with them, and a man of genius of whom it is not easy to say whether he is engaged with them or they with him' (i.e. Disraeli). This emphasis provides another respect in which Arnold's social criticism foreshadows the twentieth century, is more in keeping with it, and where it would exert greater influence.

Once more he took his point of departure from France – even the literary essays on Milton and Goethe deal with 'A French Critic on Milton', 'A French Critic on Goethe', while a third is on his old flame, George Sand. One might take for his motto the salacious beginning of Sterne's *Sentimental Journey*: 'They order this matter better in France.'

He began with the Report of the Minister of Public Instruction, bringing the figures for secondary education up to 1876. Altogether there were some 80,000 boys in inspected public schools, mainly *lycées*, and another 80,000 'in schools giving public guarantees for their efficiency'. In England there were some 20,000 under 'guaranteed' secondary instruction, i.e. public, non-private. Yet the leaders of public opinion in the newspapers remained complacent. Arnold quoted a leader that sounds like *The Times* – he used to refer to its 'Corinthian' style, now he calls it 'dithyrambic': 'All the world knows that the great middle class of this country supplies the mind, the will, and the power, for all the great and good things that have to be done, and it is not likely that that class should surrender its powers and privileges in the one case of the training of its own children. How the idea of such a scheme can have occurred to anybody, how it can have been imagined that parents and schoolmasters in the most independent and active and enlightened class of English society, how it can have been supposed that the class which has done all the great things that have been done in all departments, will beg the government to send inspectors through the schools, when it can itself command whatever advantages exist, seems almost unintelligible.'

This was the kind of attitude Arnold had to contend with. To do so more and more effectively he developed his personal style for puncturing complacency, exposing fatuity, repeating key phrases until they caught public attention and aroused public discussion. Of course he provoked intense irritation and gathered unpopularity from many quarters. This did not deter him; he was on sure ground, and he was right. His contempt for his opponents was in itself a moral support, his very superciliousness, irony and banter weapons against their humourless and earnest obtuseness. They could refrain from giving him recognition or promotion, but they could not suppress him.

Their complacency he directly confronted – may almost be said to have insulted: 'If there is one need more crying than another, it is the need of the English middle class to be rescued from a defective type of religion, a narrow range of intellect and knowledge, a stunted sense of beauty, a low standard of manners.' He repeated the indictment. Then, 'what could do so much to deliver them and to render them happier, as to give them proper education, public education . . . to make them a class homogeneous, intelligent, civilised.' Instead of that, they were content with their separate types of Creakle's and Dotheboys' academies, 'schools for the licensed victuallers, schools for the commercial travellers, schools for the Wesleyans, schools for the Quakers' – what could be more hurtful to the self-esteem of these last, temperance advocates, than to put them on a level with licensed victuallers? Their complacency was fortified by 'royal dukes and ministerial earls still found to go down and bless the young institution, and to glorify the energy and self-reliance of the commercial travellers and the licensed victuallers'. In all the twenty-two objectives specified in the Liberal party's recent statement of its aims the subject of education was not even mentioned: 'The newspapers never touch the subject' – he meant constructively; 'both upper and middle class appear content that their schools should stay as they are. . . . Our body of secondary schools is suffered to remain the most imperfect and unserviceable in civilised Europe, because our upper class does not care to be disturbed in its preponderance, or our middle class in its vulgarity.'

Arnold now advocated following 'the precedent of the Elementary Education Act, by requiring the provision throughout the country of a proper supply of secondary schools, with proper buildings and accommodations, at a proper fee, and with proper guarantees given by the teachers in the shape either of a university degree or of a special certificate for secondary instruction.' This was the next objective. In this year, 1879, we find him addressing the largest Working Men's College yet to be founded to 'try and interest them in founding a system of public education for the middle classes, on the ground that the working class suffered by not having a more civilised middle class to rise into, if they *do* rise. You may imagine the difficulty and delicacy of urging it in a public meeting in a provincial town [Ipswich], where half the audience will be middle class.'

Thus was public opinion alerted and shaped to receive in time the great Act of 1902.

CHAPTER 7

Social Criticism and Politics

WRITING TO HIS MOTHER on Christmas Day 1867, Arnold said that his reading of both Aristotle and Plato and the New Testament 'has brought Papa very much to my mind again'. Dr Arnold had been 'the only deeply religious man who had the necessary culture' to keep abreast of the modern movement of mind in theology, particularly German. It is true that Dr Arnold had a more European frame of mind and sympathies than Newman and the Tractarians – though it is useless to speculate where that would have carried him if he had lived: probably more into history. His son went on, 'then I never touch on considerations about *the State* without feeling myself on his ground.' He felt himself increasingly now to be his father's continuator: 'I like to bring before my mind the course and scope of his labours, and to try and connect my own with them. Perhaps the change of times and modes of action being allowed for, my scope is not so different from his as you and I often think.'

Next year, he was writing on his birthday, Christmas Eve, 'now I am within one year of Papa's age when he ended his life; and how much he seems to have put into it, and to what ripeness of character he had attained! Everything has seemed to come together to make this year the beginning of a new time to me: the gradual settlement of my own thought, little Basil's death, and then my dear, dear Tommy's.' Basil was but a child of two; Tom, the eldest son, was sixteen: always something of an invalid, he was yet a cherished companion for his father. 'Tommy's death in particular was associated with several awakening and epoch-making things.' The father took comfort from reading Isaiah – a favourite from henceforth. 'All these things point to a new beginning, yet it may well be that I am near my end, as Papa was at my age, but without Papa's ripeness, and that there will be little time to carry far the new beginning. But that is all the more reason for carrying it as far as one can, and as earnestly as one can, while one lives.'

This is the mood in which Arnold was writing *Culture and Anarchy*, his most significant prose-work, the central concern of his mind from which branched out his thought on society and education, on one hand, culture and (increasingly) religion on the other. With this feeling of a new phase in his life, he had in fact twenty years in which to carry forward his father's work, in changed times and modes of action, preaching to a new generation, the later Victorians. In estimating his work we have always to keep that background, those conditions, in mind: poetry to some extent transcends time, prose not.

Arnold, as we have seen, stood out as a practical man among Victorian writers, with his feet on the ground of all those pavements he trod in the course of his career as inspector of schools. And his journeyings gave him a wider conspectus of actual social conditions over the country than others had. He did not much care for fruitless metaphysical speculations, the futile logomachies of Plato's *Theaetetus*: 'The being in contact with the main stream of human life is of more moment for a man's total spiritual growth, and for his bringing to perfection the gifts committed to him, than any speculative opinions which he may hold or think he holds.'

He put forward a common-sense description, rather than a definition, of what he meant by culture, and as a practical objective for the improvement of the society of his day: 'culture being a pursuit of our total perfection by means of getting to know, on all the matters which most concern us, the best which has been thought and said in the world; and through this knowledge, turning a stream of fresh and free thought upon our stock notions and habits, which we now follow staunchly but mechanically.' In other words, a free flowing stream of *criticism* – a really significant application of the word. More important than merely external criticism, Arnold recommended it as 'an inward operation', an operation of the spirit. His Note-Books reveal that so far from being a Pharisee concerned merely with externals and preaching to others, he pursued from this time of new beginning an inner spiritual life, practising what he preached, a constant endeavour towards the ideal of moral perfection. More than most, more than any of his fellow-writers in that age, he conquered himself. There never had been the least baseness in his nature, he had always been gentle; now he underwent the ills and sufferings of life with stoical courage and submission to fate and with increase of kindness and goodness.

His own inner life was governed by striving towards an ideal of moral perfection; but this was not to achieve the negative satisfaction of 'the obvious faults of our animality', for example, the repression of sex upon which Protestantism set such exaggerated store – useful as this was for generating energy. Arnold noticed the exaggerated concern which the Hebraising tendency of the time, i.e. Biblical Protestantism, had with the notion of Sin – we should say a perfect mania. His own concern was the positive one of 'the peace and satisfaction which are reached as we draw near to complete spiritual perfection, and not merely to moral perfection, or rather to relative moral perfection'. This was his inner governor; we can trace the steps of his secret pilgrimage, unknown to others, in his Note-Books. His conduct in the world was in accordance.

His emphasis on inner cultivation was directed against the Victorian worship of machinery, the triumphs of the mechanical; individualism and 'do as you like' as the prevailing rule of society; private property as an absolute principle, hardly at all mitigated by the corrective of the state – indeed, general opposition to the intervention of the state in the interests of society; the religion of inequality, in Gladstone's phrase. Arnold described himself as a Liberal, 'yet I am a Liberal tempered by experience, reflexion, and renouncement; and I am, above all, a believer in culture.' Elsewhere, he called himself a Liberal of the future, rather than of the present. This was very pointed, when one considers the parochial concerns of the time with church-rates, church-burials, marriage with a deceased wife's sister, which he constantly held up to derision. His concern for Liberalism was loftier and wider. We have observed his campaign for middle-class education, his concern for its 'bad civilisation'; he now broadened his plea for an increasing measure of social equality. This was looking into the future with a vengeance, for in his own age practically all opinion was opposed to the idea – in his book he quotes from leaders like Disraeli, Gladstone and his friend Froude. Once more we see Arnold pitting himself against the dominant view, taking the Other Side. By now it had become his habit and inspiration – and a very salutary one, considering the strength of the current against him. But it meant that he was 'an unpopular author', as he complained.

He asserted that 'men of culture are the true apostles of equality' – in this sense: 'the great men of culture are those who have had a passion for diffusing, for making prevail, for carrying from one end of society to the other, the best knowledge, the best ideas of their time; who have laboured to divest knowledge of all that was harsh, uncouth, difficult, abstract, professional, exclusive; to humanise it, to make it efficient outside the clique of the cultivated and learned, yet still remaining the *best* knowledge and thought of the time.' This was indeed a most desirable objective, and we note how much of it goes against the pedantic, the academic in the pejorative sense of the word. It is amusing that the loftiest poet of the age, the most widely cultivated, was not afraid to be a popularizer. Himself an élitist above all (to use a nasty contemporary cliché), he took steps to issue popular editions of his books, and to provide popular readings – from Wordsworth, the Book of Isaiah, and so forth – for schools.

His mission in *Culture and Anarchy* is essentially directed to the middle class, as in all his work. Himself a middle-class man, he realized that 'so far as a man has genius he takes himself out of the category of class altogether, to become simply a man.' Transcending the limitations of his own class he does not think in terms of its clichés, as ordinary folk do. He points out that each class has its own type of literary organ and culture. He repeats his charge that the aristocracy of the time had no concern for ideas: 'One has often wondered whether upon the whole earth there is anything so unintelligent, so unapt to perceive how the world is really going, as an ordinary young Englishman of our upper class. Ideas he has not, and neither has he that seriousness of our middle class, which is the great strength of this class.' One is bound to ask, in fairness, whether they were any worse than elsewhere? – the aristocracy abroad was even less responsibly minded. Arnold's chief weakness was that he was not an historian; hence his historical generalizations are often vague, wide of the mark; it is the more remarkable how perceptive he can be.

There is, for example, his preference for the Renaissance influence as against the Reformation, of which the Victorians made such a cult, with its rebarbative heroes, Luther, Calvin, John Knox, the Protestant martyrs. Arnold remarks on 'the check given to the Renaissance by Puritanism'. If he had been an historian he might have diagnosed the disastrous retrogression in civilization engendered by the conflict between Catholicism and Protestantism – it set back the clock in Europe for more than a century. Alas, this is the form that human events on any large scale take in history. Instead of the humane, intelligent, middle-of-the-road moderation and tolerance of Erasmus – the sharpest and most civilized intellect of them all – without dogma and little use for doctrine, except the simple following of Christ's message to the inner spirit: instead of that, mutual slaughter, burnings and hangings, in the name of nonsense-concepts (Transubstantiation, Justification by Faith, etc.), and much of France and Germany laid waste by religious wars.

In *Culture and Anarchy* Arnold develops his two leading concepts, of the Hebraising and Hellenic strains, which he applied in subsequent writings. By Biblical Hebraising he meant the Protestant, especially the Puritan, emphasis on morals and conduct, with its mania about Sin; by the Hellenic strain, he meant the aim 'to find the intelligible law of things, to see them in their true nature' – he might have added the impulse towards beauty. Arnold was no aesthete, but a moralist himself, though a rational and enlightened one. At least the Hellenic strain made for intelligence in all spheres; the Hebraic, urging righteousness and good conduct (however little exemplified in the outrageous behaviour of the Puritans towards the Church and to the bishops trying to inculcate decency and order), had its social utility in building up backbone, generating the energy which defeated Spain, founded New England and released the dynamism of Oliver Cromwell.

But England had had a surfeit of Hebraism and the Bible – Arnold rightly deplored 'the long exclusive predominance of Hebraism'. Puritanism had won twice over in England – quite apart from Scotland – in the seventeenth century, and again in the nineteenth. It really dominated the tone of the age, the glum and serious side of it, the moral earnestness. Of its foremost prophet, Carlyle, Arnold spitted him with his comment that he spent his life preaching earnestness to a nation that already had too much of it – and not enough of other things, Hellenic values.

Puritanism was essentially a middle-class phenomenon, socially considered – though others elsewhere might exemplify it: *there* was its heart and home. The immense increase in the numbers and power of the middle class that accompanied the Industrial Revolution had meant a vast reinforcement of the Puritan strain, particularly in its Nonconformist forms, with Wesleyan and Primitive Methodism added to the older Dissenting sects, Congregationalists, Baptists, Paedo-Baptists, what not. So Arnold aimed his campaign at them: 'Certainly we are no enemies of the Nonconformists; for, on the contrary, which [sc. what] we aim at is their perfection.' What, in effect, could be more insulting – or, to use one of their own terms, more justified?

He went on to specify their 'narrowness, one-sidedness, incompleteness', their 'provinciality', their need for 'a more full and harmonious development of their humanity'. No wonder Arnold aroused so much controversy – quite as much as his father, though so different a man – and was so much attacked; or that Gladstone could never award him public recognition, since he depended so largely on Nonconformist votes. Perhaps this was not the worst of it. Arnold committed over and over the offence of laughing at sacred Nonconformist phenomena, the horrors of Moody and Sankey revivalism, a very 'horrid thing' if it had not been so ludicrous; the thousands of upturned faces gaping at the antics of Spurgeon in his tabernacle. (My great-uncle and -aunt travelled all the way from Cornwall to hear their paragon at the City Temple.) But the day of that kind of thing is mostly over: the religion of the people today – since the people must have a religion – is television.

It is true historically that the Church of England carries – or has carried – broadly the character of the English people: 'The Nonconformist is not in contact with the main current of national life, like the member of an establishment.' Arnold realized how fortunate the Church was to have retained its historic tradition, its catholicity, its forms and ceremonies, its institutionalism – instead of placing all its hope in doctrines as outmoded as the Westminster Confession of the Puritans. He brought home, as hardly anyone has done, the good effect upon the individual of 'a Church which is historical as the state itself is historical, and whose order, ceremonies, and monuments reach, like those of the state, far beyond any fancies and devisings of ours'. He meant the proper effect of liturgy and traditional formularies as against the posturings of the individual preacher, the 'personality-cult' of a Spurgeon – or, for that matter, of a Frank Buchman or a Billy Graham (the one so attached to Himmler, the other to Nixon).

Arnold was all in favour of order and tradition – not, in his case, for aesthetic but for moral reasons: 'Without order there can be no society, and without society there can be no human perfection.' This has its bearing, a still more urgent message for today – if there were anyone likely to listen to it. The logical end of liberalism is the anarchy spreading all round us; when anarchy reaches the point of breaking a social order down, it is likely to produce the kind of reaction that no liberal likes. Arnold well appreciated the danger – and was shortly to be corroborated by the Paris Commune of 1871: 'Because a State in which law is authoritative and sovereign, a firm and settled course of public order is requisite, if man is to bring to maturity anything precious or lasting now, or to found anything precious and lasting for the future. Thus, in our eyes, the very framework and exterior order of the State, whoever may administer the State, is sacred; and culture is the most resolute enemy of anarchy, because of the great hopes and designs for the State which culture teaches us to nourish.'

Arnold does not pursue the original thought, the most pressing concern for today, which he here opens up – the dependence of any real culture on an ordered society. Obviously Pop Culture goes very well with Anarchy – the erosion of the 'precious and lasting' values and achievements that Arnold cared for, which are all that a cultivated man thinks worth caring for. But Arnold's emphasis on the state was not welcome to the Victorians – it was thought Continental, one more un-English thing about him. This was in marked contrast with Tennyson, who is cited by name in *Culture and Anarchy* for his celebration of 'the great broad-shouldered genial Englishman', with his 'sense of duty', his 'reverence for the laws', and his 'patient force' and, Arnold adds, his contempt for other, less broad-shouldered nations.

We see why Tennyson became popular, Arnold not.

Arnold ends by saying that both despondency and violence are forbidden to the man of culture – all very well in the security of the nineteenth century; but as the tide of violence rises in the twentieth century there is more and more reason to despond.

In these years Arnold carried his banner into journalism with a series of letters and replies in the *Pall Mall Gazette*, published as *Friendship's Garland*. The letters, with their strictures upon England, were supposed to be by one Arminius von Thunder-ten-Tronck, a name out of *Candide*, with Arnold answering on behalf of England (!) under his own name. It makes a very odd work of Victorian banter, which has had its appeal to some people of Victorian tastes, but not to us. Nor did Arnold himself ever republish it. It is indeed a topical work, mostly of ephemeral interest, though a few things stand out.

Arnold carries forward his career of needling the public and showing up Victorian assumptions. Was more and more liberty the test of greatness for a nation? What about Bismarck's Germany, united by force, now victorious over France, the most powerful country in Europe? Is the worship of property to have no bounds put to it? Prussia, from the time of Stein, had assigned bounds to it in the interest of the state. In place of progress towards anarchy, obedience was inculcated. Arnold quoted some choice specimens of complacent self-congratulation from *The Times*, *Telegraph* and elsewhere – for example, 'the lesson, of which England has been the special teacher, that national greatness and wealth are to be prized only in so far as they ensure the freedom of the individual citizen, and the right of all to join in free debate'. If there was something in this, it was not the way to put it.

Arnold responded with his best invention in the book, the very Victorian Mr Bottles: 'a Radical of the purest water; quite one of the Manchester School. He was one of the earliest free-traders; he has always gone as straight as an arrow about Reform; he is an ardent voluntary in every possible line, opposed the Ten Hours' Bill [limiting hours of work in factories]; was one of the leaders of the Dissenting opposition which smashed up the Education clauses of Sir James Graham's Factory Act; and he paid the whole expenses of a most important church-rate contest out of his own pocket. And, finally, he looks forward to marrying his deceased wife's sister.' Arnold regarded with derision the fixation of Liberal Nonconformists on their grievances about paying church-rates and not being allowed to marry their deceased wife's sister, when they should be campaigning for other and better things – the proper education of their children for one.

Politics were in an uncertain state in the 1850s and 1860s; the aristocracy had lost the certainty of touch that led the country to defeat the French Revolution and Napoleon, when France had two or three times the population of Britain. The old ruling class had perpetually to be looking over its shoulder at what the middle classes and their newspapers were saying and thinking. It was not the aristocracy but the middle class that had made the Crimean War. Arnold was attacked yet once more by the *Saturday Review* for saying all this, and in his reply, 'My Countrymen', spoke out more trenchantly than ever.

The *Telegraph* described the English as 'the Imperial Race', and here was the record. Palmerston, a sprig of the aristocracy, was the darling of the middle classes – every Englishman loved a lord. At the end of his spectacular, blustering career, having begun with England 'the first power in the world's estimation, he leaves her the third. . . . It was not the aristocracy which made the Crimean war: it was the strong middle part – the constituencies. It was the strong middle part which showered abuse and threats on Germany for mishandling

Denmark; and when Germany gruffly answered, *Come and stop us*, slapped its pockets, and vowed that it had never had the slightest notion of pushing matters so far as this. It was the strong middle part which, by the voice of its favourite newspapers, kept threatening Germany with a future chastisement from France. It was the strong middle part, speaking through the same newspapers, which was full of coldness, slights, and sermons for the American Federals during their late struggle; and as soon as they had succeeded, discovered that it had always wished them well.'

In truth the Victorian middle class did not make a pretty picture. And what about the hideousness of lower-class life in the most complacent of countries? 'No-one can walk with his eyes and ears open through the poor quarters of your large towns, and not feel that your common people is at present more raw, to say the very least, less enviable-looking, further removed from civilised and humane life than the common people almost anywhere.' 'Drugged with business, your middle class seems to have its sense blunted for any stimulus besides, except religion; it has a religion narrow, unintelligent, repulsive.' Here was their round – and there followed a celebrated summing up: 'from an illiberal, dismal life at Islington to an illiberal, dismal life at Camberwell. . . . Can any life be imagined more hideous, more dismal, more unenviable? Compare it with the life of the middle class as you have seen it on the Rhine this summer, or at Lausanne, or Zürich.' And so on, no longer bantering, but taunting, belabouring.

One can only say that it was brave of him; we in our time would not dare to say such things.

Arnold realized that the incursions of men of letters into politics were not welcome to practical politicians, and – better than intellectuals in the twentieth century – how wrong their judgments of passing events were apt to be. Arnold, always apt to be on the generous side towards the lower orders, was no exception. On the Paris Commune of 1871, he wrote to his mother that it 'does not make me so angry as it does many people, because I do not think well enough of Thiers and the French upper class generally to think it very important they should win. What is certain is that all the seriousness, clear-mindedness, and settled purpose is on the side of the Reds. I suspect they will win, and we shall see for a time the three or four chief cities of France Socialistic free cities, in an attitude independent and hostile to the more backward and conservative country.'

What a misjudgment this was! Arnold always nourished the middle-class illusion that the working class was given to 'ideas', that they were more generous than other classes – there was some truth in this, but only so long as they had nothing to be selfish about. What the Paris Commune showed above all was that the main idea of the working class was destruction: it destroyed or set on fire what it could of the monuments of culture of the past, Renaissance buildings like the Hôtel de Ville, palaces like the Tuileries. Just as the French Revolutionaries had destroyed innumerable châteaux, works of art and relics of the civilization they were incapable of. Arnold was too generous, though at the same time far-sighted: 'the Paris convulsion is an explosion of that fixed resolve of the working class to count for something and *live*, which is destined to make itself so much felt in the coming time, and to disturb so much which dreamed it would last for ever.' *It*, however, did last for a century more; there was not a hope of the Commune winning at the time, or of the whole French nation putting up with the dictatorship of the Parisian proletariat or its frenzy of destruction. And if Arnold had been more of an aesthete he would have minded the senseless destruction more.

At home he regarded his writings as sapping the influence of political Dissent, while he continued to earn his living by inspecting their schools. He complained of the drudgery of his life: 'after all, it is absurd that all the best of my days should be taken up with matters which thousands of other people could do just as well as I, and that what I have a special turn for doing I should have no time for.' It was the poetry that was sacrificed. He must have thought of this when he went back this year, 1871, to Thun with its memories of Marguerite. Arnold took on his old guide again, hale and hearty at sixty.

The drudgery went on; so too the prose. In 1879, as we have seen, he put together *Mixed Essays*, which had two important pieces. In 'Democracy' he showed that he understood the aristocratic attitude towards politics from the inside – no doubt from his apprenticeship with Lansdowne. What he says is most helpful to the understanding of nineteenth-century government – historians of the period have not profited from his observation so much as they might. He is explaining that aristocrats had no wish for a strong executive or taste for very active administration: 'It is a disposition proper to them as great personages, not as ministers; and as they are great personages for their whole life, while they may probably be ministers but for a very short time, the instinct of their social condition avails more with them than the instinct of their official function. To administer as little as possible, to make its weight felt in foreign affairs rather than in domestic, to see in ministerial station rather the means of power and dignity than a means of searching and useful administrative activity, is the natural tendency of an aristocratic executive.' He concluded that aristocrats did not make good administrators.

This is not only excellently observed, but it gives us a clue to the frequent ministerial chops and changes of the period, many of which seem frivolous in retrospect. The fact is that ministerial office did not add much to grandees like the Duke of Devonshire or the Marquis of Lansdowne, with their thousands of broad acres in England, Scotland and Ireland, and their interests and responsibilities as such. Lansdowne refused to be Foreign Secretary, Hartington twice refused the Premiership; Derby infuriated Disraeli by missing chances of office for the Tories and his refusal to come to London, though leader of the party, for months on end. It was a parvenu, like Disraeli, who hungered for office and power; great aristocrats would leave office at the drop of a hat.

There were exceptions, like Palmerston, who was an able administrator too. Aristocratic incompetence in administration had been shown up in a lurid light in the Crimean War. The really able administrators were middle-class men like Peel and Gladstone.

Arnold was no less understanding of the impulse that drove

democracy to make its demands. The impulse of life, he said, is *to affirm one's own essence*; and 'this movement of democracy, like other operations of nature, merits properly neither blame nor praise.' Dominant opinion at the time was unsympathetic to its progress; not so Arnold. He considered the approach towards equality, 'at any rate a certain reduction of inequalities, a natural instinctive demand of that impulse which drives society as a whole'. To live in a society of superiors might be good discipline, but was discouraging to the faculties of the inferior: 'Can it be denied that, to be heavily overshadowed, to be profoundly insignificant, has on the whole a depressing and benumbing effect on the character?'

This was a salutary reflexion upon Victorian society, with its insufferable arrogance on the part of the aristocracy towards the middle class, and of the upper classes as a whole towards working people. Arnold himself had none of this arrogance; he was indeed supercilious or, rather, genuinely superior. In inspecting the schools of the people he was noted to be exceptionally gentle and kind to the children.

What are we to conclude today? What is the relevance of what this acute observer of Victorian society has to say to ours?

His emphasis was wholly right – besides being generous – for his age. Today, conditions have completely changed with the social revolution we are going through. The inflexion that needs urging today is the opposite one. The first charge upon the resources of our society, rightly enough, is the people at large. It is *their* society; very well, it is for them to do their best for it, not to wreck their own show by selfish and irresponsible demands upon it. Masses of the highest-paid workers, through the monopoly power of their trade unions, show themselves quite as selfish and predatory as eighteenth-century oligarchs or Edwardian society leaders – at the expense of less well-paid workers and everybody else.

'To affirm one's own essence' is a polite way of saying, what is true, that the aggressive assertion of ego is the prime impulse in the struggle for survival. But for a society to be successful and not to be torn apart or to break down, the conflicts of group-egoisms need to be co-ordinated and directed in the general interest: the great problem for democracy today.

In nineteenth-century circumstances Arnold could hardly be expected to appreciate how much really high cultural standards depend on a certain amount of inequality; or how a culturally variegated society is more propitious to artistic and intellectual creativeness than a more monochrome, let alone a one-class society (if indeed such exists, outside of primitive tribal conditions). Nor did he allow for the uses and advantages of 'social imitation', which a sociologist such as Tarde perceived the purpose of: in an hierarchical society the superior class can set good standards for those below to follow – in social service, public spirit, duty, or even culturally, artistically, intellectually.

When the great mass of men have free and equal opportunity to fulfil what they have in them, and the state itself provides equal conditions towards that end, Arnold's strictures no longer hold, his urgings are no longer necessary. His genius, his inner illumination, told him the truth, as in 'Rugby Chapel':

> *Most men eddy about*
> *Here and there – eat and drink*
> *Chatter and love and hate,*
> *Gather and squander, are raised*
> *Aloft, are hurled in the dust,*
> *Striving blindly, achieving*
> *Nothing; and then they die –*
> *Perish; and no one asks*
> *Who or what they have been . . .*

The truth is that it is the nature of the mass of mankind to be 'profoundly insignificant'; it is an untruth to tell them otherwise. So a truer view of human nature today would be to recommend them to fulfil what they have it in them to fulfil, to the best of their ability, contentedly, without exaggerated expectations or scrabbling for more than their fair share, let alone for more than the little they have to contribute.

In his day Arnold made his contribution by putting the unpopular side, the case that needed to be put. So, too, with a conscientious writer today, when the boot is on the other foot: it is the disadvantages of mass-democracy that need to be realized, popular illusions exposed, untruths denied. Arnold was too clear-sighted to entertain illusions – he had an inkling how things might turn out. 'The real danger is that it [democracy] will have far too much its own way. . . . The difficulty for democracy is how to find and keep high ideals.' In his own day he was rather too generous in his expectations: he thought that, as opposed to the aristocracy, democracy was given to ideas!

On the contrary, what people are like when emancipated from restraints may be seen today in the civilized exchanges of Northern Ireland, or the self-evident altruism of the trade unions in Britain. Arnold saw the limitation that exists in the nature of things upon freedom of opinion as an absolute end: 'It is a very great thing to be able to think as you like; but after all an important question remains: *what* you think.' This, with the mass of mankind, is and always has been, as the historian knows, largely nonsense.

Arnold was weakest in historical generalization – where his father had the advantage, as an historian; but he did perceive 'the mind-deadening influence of a narrow Biblism' upon the middle class and could point out, as the Protestant Dr Arnold could not, that from the seventeenth century it *entered the prison of Puritanism, and had the key turned upon its spirit therefore for two hundred years.* This was nearer to Newman than to Dr Arnold. His son was the only writer, so far as I know, to indicate the cultural and artistic losses under the Commonwealth, the sale of the King's pictures, of tapestries, statuary, vestments from the churches. He could have gone much further – the dispersal of the cathedral and collegiate choirs, the destruction of organs and music, the ripping up of brasses, defacing of tombs, etc., apart from the devastation of the Civil War brought on by militant Puritanism.

'There is nothing more unlovely and unamiable than Milton the Puritan disputant.' Arnold deplored equally the tedious religious disputes that were the delight of the Victorian middle class: 'Those who offer us the Puritan type of life offer us a religion not true, the claims of intellect and knowledge not satisfied, the claim of beauty not satisfied, the claim of manners not satisfied.' He extends his indictment of the 'religion of inequality' to nineteenth-century society as a whole, with its 'natural and necessary effect, under present circumstances, of materialising our upper class, vulgarising our middle class, and brutalising our lower class'. With the consequences for this last he was more familiar than most writers, from his own observation: 'The greater the inequality the more marked is its bad action upon the middle and lower classes. In Scotland the landed aristocracy fills the scene; the other classes are more squeezed back and effaced. And the social civilisation of the lower middle class and of the poorest class in Scotland is an example of the consequences. Compared with the same class even in England, the Scottish lower middle class is most visibly *less* well-bred, *less* careful in personal habits and in social conventions, *less* refined. Let anyone who doubts it go . . . and observe the shopkeepers and the middle class in Dumbarton, and Greenock, and Gourock, and the places along the mouth of the Clyde. And for the poorest class, who that has seen it can ever forget the hardly human horror, the abjection and uncivilisedness of Glasgow?'

Again one is astonished at Arnold's outspokenness.

From Scotland to Ireland: with the Liberal victory of 1880, Ireland became the chief problem for government; expectations were aroused which could not be fulfilled in the existing circumstances, with the balance of forces in society translated into politics. In the Irish question, as in international politics, only the facts of power counted, whatever anybody *said*. Arnold was drawn into discussion since it was the leading issue in all men's minds, or on their lips – a better word for it; but he was the more concerned because his brother-in-law, Forster, became Chief Secretary for Ireland, the most dangerous post in politics – his life was constantly aimed at, his successor, Lord Frederick Cavendish, murdered. In Irish circumstances the gospel of 'sweetness and light' – though more needed there than anywhere (ironically, the phrase was Swift's) – was out of place, irrelevant and futile.

The essays which Arnold addressed to the subject, republished in 1882 in *Irish Essays*, had been 'received with no great favour'. The essays are indeed feeble, for what could anyone offer that was useful in such circumstances? There were only these alternatives: either rule Ireland by force, or get out. Ireland could always have been subjugated by superior force, if the English and Scotch thought it worth it, and secondly, if they were united in carrying it through. Holding Ireland meant maintaining the Protestant Ascendancy of landlords and Established Church. Gladstone had removed one pillar of the fabric by disestablishing the Church of Ireland in 1869.

It might have helped to hold Ireland for decades more if the Catholic Church had then been endowed and established there instead: the Roman Church was much the best instrument for keeping people muffled and quiet. But the English Nonconformists, the mainstay of the Liberal Party, would not hear of it: *they* made it impossible to govern Ireland. They would not even permit the endowment of a Catholic university or Catholic schools, such as the Irish wanted. This was as monstrously unfair as it was unwise, as Arnold pointed out. Presbyterianism was established in Scotland, Anglicanism in England, why not Catholicism in Ireland?

Now Gladstone was chiselling away at the landlord system in Ireland, with his various Land Acts, beginning to undermine the landlords, the second pillar that had upheld the structure of society there. Arnold wrote, 'to break down the landlords in Ireland, as we have already broken down the Protestant Church there, is merely to complete the destruction of the *modus vivendi* hitherto existing for society in that country; a most imperfect *modus vivendi* indeed, but the only one practically attained there up to this time as a substitute for anarchy.' The alternative, to leave the Irish people free to dispose of their own affairs, was hardly considered feasible yet by anybody. However much a Celt may sympathize with this as an ultimate objective, the historian must admit that in the 1880s the time was not yet ripe for it, i.e. the balance of forces in the two countries would not yet permit of it.

Arnold saw more clearly than most that it was as impossible to go on governing Ireland through the landlords as through the Protestant Church. And he realized that Gladstone's Land Act would not go far to 'heal the estrangement between Ireland and England'. Well, what would? All he could offer was the vague hope that 'England and

English civilisation shall become more attractive; that we should not only *do* to Ireland something different from what we have done hitherto, but should also *be* something different.' It was a hopeless message: the Irish wanted nothing of it, simply to be, and be left to, themselves. Arnold had the awareness, in referring to the different stocks that made up Britain, always to include the Cornish. But he would no more believe that Ireland wanted a separate existence than that 'Scotland, Wales, or Cornwall would have either to be governed as Crown colonies for the future, or to be given up. I no more believe the despondent observers [about the Union of Ireland with Britain] than I should believe them if they assured me that Scotland, Wales, or Cornwall were fatally and irresistibly drifting to a miserable separation from England.' In fact, the despondent observers were right; and even his certainty about Scotland, Wales, and Cornwall is not without question today.

Arnold was in favour of getting rid of bad landlords – as Swift had been in favour of making absentee landlords reside, in days when the Protestant-English interest in Ireland could have been strengthened instead of sabotaged by sheer, short-sighted selfishness in England. Now it was too late. No amount of sweetness and light was any good. Arnold was always on the side of generosity, of making concessions: it was all he had to suggest except what had now become clichés. He quoted a favourite saying: *Mansueti possidebunt terram*, which he translated, 'the gentle shall possess the earth'.

Upon which we can only ask, with the advantage of our hideous experience of the twentieth century: *Do they?*

From Ireland to America is a short step that many have taken. It was not until his last years that Arnold visited America, for the classic purpose of making money by lecture tours. He spent the winter of 1883–84 in this remunerative employment, and returned for a shorter bout in 1886. He needed the money to pay the debts of his one remaining son, Dick, a feeble specimen who achieved nothing in his short life, except the friendship of Elgar. Richard Penrose Arnold was musical, like the eldest boy Tom: this did not come from the Arnold side of the family. Elgar devoted one of the 'Enigma Variations' to R.P.A., where his character is suggested. He was largely self-taught, and given to evading difficulties; but he had real feeling for the mystery of music, which he concealed behind a good deal of whimsical badinage.

We do not need to follow Arnold's opinions about America, expressed at large in his correspondence. To the end of his life he saw the United States (he much preferred Canada) as just an extension of England across the Atlantic, with much the same characteristics writ larger, and even more vulgar. Indeed his opinions may be summed up in that one word. When he says, not infrequently, that he fears the spread of 'Americanisation', he means democratization and vulgarization. He saw the Americans as mainly a middle-class nation, at any rate dominated by its middle class, without an aristocracy, and therefore characterized by all the defects he had so often underlined in the middle class at home.

This was a very inadequate view. For there was, and is, an élite in America, though – almost submerged as it is by the democratic humbug coming down from Jefferson, cloudy thinking that has led the nation astray in the hard realities of the twentieth century – it hardly dares to admit its own existence. Where Arnold's real sympathies lay may be seen from the American figures he admired: Washington and Hamilton. To these he might have added Henry Adams, if he had known him, Henry James, Santayana, Eliot. He did not appreciate the plebeian Lincoln, to whom he preferred the soldierly Grant – a mistake.

One must make a sharp distinction between American mass-civilization and the cultivated élite, always a minority everywhere. Nowhere is the distinction sharper, though elided by the democratic ideology to which America conforms. Unless one realizes this from the outset, one does American culture a grave injustice; for the strictures applied by foreign observers, the rude remarks about vulgarity and commonness – Arnold summed it up as *das Gemeine* – true enough of the masses, are true of the masses everywhere else, and are no more true of the American élite than anywhere else. Americans do themselves a grave injustice by subscribing to democratic humbug and refusing to recognize the distinction.

Arnold had an important following in America: his poetry, his criticism, his religious writings – particularly *Literature and Dogma*, he found – were as much appreciated by cultivated people there as at home. He had a wider influence in education. He found that everyone knew the name of his father, whose influence had been a prime one upon the American counterparts of the English Public Schools. (One sees this recognized in Louis Auchincloss's distinguished novel, *The Rector of Justin*.) Garfield, later President, cited Arnold's Report of 1868 in Congress, for its argument that 'the public school for the people must rest on the municipal organization of the country.'

With the Americans, the most generous of all peoples, 'no other foreign critic, and perhaps few native ones, have acquired such a reputation and exercised such a palpable influence on American culture.' Perhaps it helped a bit, too, that he was so captious about the English. Henry James was a notable admirer, especially of Arnold's civility and gentlemanly good manners in dispute (though we are rather shocked by his outspokenness): 'in prose and verse the idol of my previous years'. When James was asked to reply to Arnold's unfavourable view of America, he pleaded that he could not, 'it was so true and carried me so along with it.' Arnold and James were agreed in finding the America of their time *uninteresting*: this was wrong of them, but they meant culturally uninteresting. Nothing that Arnold wrote was so wounding as the famous passage in James's *Hawthorne*, where he dwelt on the bare and bleak landscape without cathedrals, palaces, châteaux, Florentine villas or Oxford colleges; without an ancient aristocracy with its tradition and manners and *douceur de vivre*; in those days without galleries and museums, pictures and opera; without the rich and colourful layers of social life upon which the artist's imagination could feed.

What James says of Arnold's literary criticism is illuminating in the perspective of the time: 'All criticism is better, lighter, more sympathetic, more informed in consequence of certain things he has said.' It lights up for us the lugubrious, heavy-handed state of criticism which he displaced and formed a better school. His was a prime influence with the new Humanists, such as Irving Babbitt, earlier this century. T. S. Eliot was a devoted disciple: he himself told me that in his younger years he could quote whole slabs of Arnold's prose, and it is not difficult to discern whence the pupil derived a certain tone of voice and manner. More important, Eliot followed precisely Arnold's pattern from literary to political and religious criticism, and on to the problems of culture and society. A critic has summed up, perhaps too generously: 'the mutual congenialities between Arnold and America can be multiplied: the idea that "races" must be conciliated to enrich one another; the ultimate belief that morality and conduct *are* more important than intelligence or knowledge; the indifference to the fine arts; and the love of nature.'

Arnold had a generous welcome everywhere he went, was treated *en prince* and met all the leading figures. But he was a poor lecturer – he said of his Oxford lectures that he 'would not like Papa to hear' him; he read his script in a monotonous way, without emphasis, he had not a strong voice, and was inaudible. President Grant said to his wife that they had paid their money to hear the British lion roar, and since they could not hear him they might as well go. A Middle West journalist described him, rather convincingly, as like an elderly macaw pecking at grapes on a trellis. But his lectures, and what he had to say, were widely taken up, commented upon and discussed in the press. He had never met anything like the American press: he was pursued to distraction and fled in dismay. Considering what he was, what he said and how he said it, he was treated with courtesy, forbearance and respect.

Let us take a few snapshots of Arnold *en route*, from his Letters. In October 1883 he is writing in 'a delightful, poky, dark, exclusive, little old club of the Dutch families in New York. It is the only place where I have found peace' – not the Knickerbocker Club, however. He was to be taken to hear the notorious Henry Ward Beecher preach – whom he had described at home as 'a heated barbarian'; and to be taken for 'a spin' behind two famous American trotters – such as Churchill's grandfather, Leonard Jerome, used to drive up and down Fifth Avenue. Thence up the Hudson to the Delanos', presumably Hyde Park, the cosy English-style country house of Franklin Roosevelt's domineering Delano mother: 'It was like staying with the Rothschilds.' He observed the freedom from constraint among middle-class people, 'the buoyancy and enjoyment everywhere, which confirmed me in all I have said about the way in which the aristocratic class acts as an *incubus* upon our middle class at home.' We are amused to note, however, that Mr Delano 'grumbled because everyone took a right of way through his grounds just as they pleased.' There are such disadvantages in a democracy.

Arnold's main lecture, 'Numbers', was much discussed everywhere. The theme of it was that the majority were 'unsound', and that there was virtue only in the 'Remnant' – the phrase came from Isaiah: it meant simply the élite, and it reverberated – Arnold was too proud of Disraeli's compliment upon his 'great achievement' of launching phrases. Effective as they were in his day, their repetition in his writings became wearisome. At Boston 'the people were all full of Papa, and the little boys were reading *Tom Brown* with delight.' As we have seen, he found that *Literature and Dogma* had made a marked impression, and was warmly welcomed by ministers of religion, who regarded the book as having a conservative tendency: 'The force of mere convention is much less strong here than in England.'

His second lecture, on the subject of Emerson, was a rather ambivalent tribute to the sage. At Concord Arnold met his widow, a formidable New England dragon: 'brought up a strict Calvinist, and never approved her husband's views'. Arnold's portrait of her reminds me of a similar New England harpy, who said to me, grinding her dentures, 'I don't wish to hate people, but I must uphold virtue.' In Washington Arnold had a glimpse of the South, and 'if ever I come back to America, it will be to see more of the South.' Certainly English people feel more at home there, more relaxed, slower-paced, more genial.

In the Middle West he comments on the absence of the picturesque – 'the rarest of things here, and the people have even less of the artist feeling than we have.' At Chicago Arnold quotes a recognizable description of himself: 'he has harsh features, supercilious manners, parts his hair down the middle, wears a single eyeglass and ill-fitting clothes.' He was much interested by St Louis with its (then) considerable French element, 'descended from the French of Louisiana', and a large German population, complete with beer-gardens and singing halls. He does not mention T. S. Eliot's grandfather, who had left New England to found Washington University and spread Unitarian light, if not sweetness, in that dark region.

In Canada – 'I would sooner be a poor priest in Quebec than a rich hog-merchant in Chicago' – he was invited to stay at Ottawa, by the grandson of his old patron, Lansdowne, who was Governor-General. When he got home to England in the spring, he sent to his French friend, Fontanès, his lecture on 'Numbers', with the explanation that it was expedient in America, 'where plain truth is not palatable, to lead up to the dangers of America through those of England and France'. He had managed to express a number of plain truths, but were they likely to be more palatable anywhere else?

As well as his lectures, Arnold wrote several articles about America, which have only recently been republished; he was as usual asked to write a book on the subject. His little volume, *Discourses in America*, was a favourite with him, as parents' weakest bantlings are apt to be. The leading essay, 'Numbers', has nothing that he had not said before, and one notices a certain failure of confidence with regard to the future, perhaps the tiredness of one within a few years of his end. The best thing in the book is the quotation from Bishop Butler: 'things and actions are what they are; and the consequences of them will be what they will be: why then should we desire to be deceived?' Arnold never tired of quoting this piece of *désabusé* realism in his last writings. He warned that 'moral causes govern the standing and the falling of states.' There is some truth in this, but they depend for their effect upon social arrangements, and the structure, character, and institutions of the state.

The lecture on 'Emerson', heard with expectation in New England, began with Arnold's memorable description of Newman preaching in St Mary's – a bewitching memory: how they all remembered him, even Froude who went over to Carlyle! Arnold always retained something like veneration for his father's old *bête noire*, now a Cardinal, though he regarded Newman's 'solution for the doubts and difficulties which beset men's minds today' as 'frankly impossible'.

However, Arnold had attended the princely reception for the Cardinal at Norfolk House on his return from Rome: 'He was in state at one end of the room, with the Duke of Norfolk on one side of him and a chaplain on the other; people filed before him as before the Queen, dropping on their knees when they were presented and kissing his hand. That old mountebank, Lord—— , dropped on his knees [though not one of the faithful], and mumbled the Cardinal's hand like a piece of cake. I only made a deferential bow, and Newman took my hand in both of his and was charming. He said, "I ventured to tell the Duchess I should like to see you". One had to move on directly, for there was a crowd of devotees waiting. But I am very glad to have seen him.'

What would Dr Arnold have thought of it all?

Though Arnold now preferred Emerson to Carlyle, his treatment of the sage of Concord must have sounded deflating of their paragon to New England ears: 'One of the legitimate poets, Emerson, in my opinion, was not. His poetry is interesting, it makes one think; but it is not the poetry of one of the born poets.' 'Of not more than one or two passages in Emerson's poetry can it, I think, be truly said that they stand everpresent in the memory of even many lovers of English poetry.' His verse 'lacks directness; it lacks concreteness; it lacks energy. His grammar is often embarrassed; in particular, the want of clearly marked distinction between the subject and the object of his sentence' – perhaps, as in his thought! 'But I go further, and say that I do not place him among the great writers, the great men of letters.' 'Emerson cannot, I think, be called with justice a great philosophical writer. He cannot build; his arrangement of philosophical ideas has no progress in it, no evolution; he does not construct a philosophy.'

What, indeed, is left of poor Emerson after this? Arnold confessed that he much preferred Hawthorne: his taste was not at fault. But was it to hear this that cultivated New England had paid its lecture fees? This was what it got.

When he got back he denied that he had said that America was vulgar. Of course he had, and had always thought it. But so is everywhere else, if you look at the populace: America is no exception.

That is what the word 'vulgar' means: *vulgus* means populace. And, as Cicero says crisply: *non est consilium in vulgo, non ratio* – there is no judgment in the populace, nor reason. If cultivated Americans wish to deny the aspersion on their culture, then they should give up their democratic camouflage. Washington and Hamilton did not subscribe to it; Henry Adams had none of it, nor Henry James, nor Santayana, nor Eliot, nor Samuel Eliot Morison; only the second-rate stand or, rather, fall by it.

Arnold had long before expressed his fears: 'I see a wave of more than American *vulgarity*, moral, intellectual, and social, preparing to break over us.' He agreed with Renan – a kindred spirit, a fellow Celt – as to the vulgarity of manners of countries committing themselves to popular education for 'serious higher instruction'. In 'Equality' he had written the warning that, 'in America, perhaps, we see the disadvantages of having social equality before there has been any high standard of social life and manners formed.' To expect any such thing from the populace was to ask for the impossible.

Arnold saw in America the same faults he had often descanted upon in Britain – not surprisingly, since he regarded America as dominated by its middle class: 'The Americans came originally, for the most part, from that great class in English society amongst whom the sense for conduct and business is much more strongly developed than the sense for beauty. If we in England were without the cathedrals, parish churches, and castles of the Catholic and feudal age, and without the houses of the Elizabethan age, but had only the towns and buildings which the rise of our middle class has created in the modern age, we should be in much the same case as the Americans.' This is why he found America fundamentally *uninteresting* – as Henry James did: 'Now the great sources of the *interesting* are distinction and beauty. Let us take the beautiful first, and consider how far it is present in American civilisation. . . .'

If Arnold had been more of an historian, he would have found more that is interesting, more to appreciate. As it was, he was able to score against American self-esteem as much as British. There was the patriotic historian Bancroft, for whom the progress of American democracy 'proceeded as uniformly and majestically as the laws of being and was as certain as the decrees of eternity'. This is the kind of thing that has maddened the French in our time, and was so much resented by a distinguished mind like de Gaulle, with the application of such shallow and callow concepts outside the bounds of the United States, in Africa or the East. They regarded the Viet Nam war as a revenge upon such ignorant presumption from such a source. Americans, said Henry Ward Beecher complacently, have 'a genius for the organisation of states'. 'Ours is the elect nation, ours is the elect nation for the age to come', preached an American reformer; 'we are the chosen people.' It might be a complacent middle-class Victorian at home speaking.

Actually Arnold was prepared to give the Americans credit, in nineteenth-century circumstances, for political and social success which the twentieth century has belied: 'A people homogeneous, a people which had to constitute itself in a modern age, and which has given to itself institutions entirely fitted for such an age' . . . Arnold did not know America at all well; but he had observed the Civil War, the most truly tragic experience of the nineteenth century. With a little more historical perception he would not have described the American people as 'homogeneous', when in fact they are riven from top to bottom between black and white. Nor would he have been so complimentary about the success of American political and social institutions if he had had the sour advantages of living through the 1960s and 1970s. He had less expectation of their educational institutions anyway, but he would have been shocked at the behaviour of students everywhere in the populist conditions of the twentieth century: 'The political problem and the social problem, the people of the United States does appear to me to have solved, or Fortune has solved it for them, with undeniable success.' Neither the 'Fortune' nor the 'success' is so evident now: what Arnold wrote reads ironically today.

In his time, as most foreigners observed, 'all this tall talk and self-glorification meets with hardly any rebuke from sane criticism over there'. It has taken a great fall of late, a *crise de conscience* throughout the nation, which should lead to an examination of its fundamental assumptions. In the nineteenth century it could be replied that this was but the Englishman writ large, or indeed the average man anywhere. But precisely: the cult of the average man is the end of civilization, in any exact or significant sense.

And the average woman? Arnold said something that no one would dare to say today: 'much may be said against the voices and intonation of American women.' Fancy his saying anything of the sort – and he such a gentleman!

Arnold liked America so little that much of what was interesting he missed: 'What people in whom the sense for beauty and fitness was quick could have invented, or could tolerate, the hideous names ending in *ville*, the Briggsvilles, Higginsvilles, Jacksonvilles, rife from Maine to Florida; the jumble of unnatural and inappropriate names everywhere?' But there is a homely propriety – and more, to those who know their historic associations – in such names as Springfield, Concord, Bull Run, New Harmony; Martha's Vine-yard, Red Cloud, or Cedar Mountain; Dearborn, Turnagain or Trouble Enough. There is beauty everywhere in the Spanish names, Monterey, San Juan de Alcalà, San Juan Capistrano, San Luìs Obispo, La Reina de los Angeles. And the original Indian names offer incomparable echoes: Nantucket, Susquehanna, Merrimack; Rappahannock, Minnehaha, Tennessee; Chattanooga, Savannah, Minnesota; Shenandoah, or Mount Monadnock, which Melville had in view from his house, and at the foot of which Willa Cather lies.

CHAPTER 8

Literature and Religion

THE 1870s WERE FILLED for Arnold by the publication of his writings on religion; it was a time of religious disputes, ritualistic disturbances, and a campaign on the part of the Nonconformists for the disestablishment of the Church of England, following upon that in Ireland. Literary folk like Saintsbury have deplored Arnold's diversion from literature; but he did not think of literature as divorced from society. He thought of literature as a vocation, with its responsibilities, and that the judgment of a man of letters had something to offer to religion. In the central work of the series he wrote, *Literature and Dogma* – a key book along with *Culture and Anarchy*, and the volume of his which appealed most to the public and sold best – he says, 'the valuable thing in letters – that is, in the acquainting oneself with the best which has been thought and said in the world – is the judgment which forms itself insensibly in a fair mind along with fresh knowledge.' To a French Protestant pastor he wrote (in French), 'in speaking of St Paul I have not spoken as a theologian, but as a man of letters disapproving of the unsatisfactory literary treatment of a great spirit. If I had spoken as a theologian no-one would have listened.'

Again we must view these works in relation to the time in which they were written and the purpose he had in mind, if we are to appreciate their place in his life's work. *St Paul and Protestantism* came first, in 1870, a work in the line of Dr Arnold which went, however, much further than the Doctor would have gone, to break wholly with Christian orthodoxy: the son ventured to disbelieve in a personal God (and earned the disapproval of an Archbishop of Canterbury). He continued with his diagnosis of the contrasting strains in Christianity, the Hebraic and the Hellenic, with a comment in his

Letters that his father would not give the province to Hellenism that he had done.

The book was prefaced with an essay on 'Puritanism and the Church of England', which might have been written by one of the Oxford Malignants, he detested the Puritans so much. He considered that Puritanism rested upon a perversion of St Paul's teaching, and he cited the Calvinist doctrine of election: 'By God's decree a certain number of angels and men are predestinated, out of God's mere free grace and love, without any foresight of faith or good works in them, to everlasting life; and others foreordained, according to the unsearchable counsel of his will, whereby he extends or withholds mercy as he pleases, to everlasting death.' We have no difficulty in perceiving that this is a tissue of non-sense propositions; the explanation of the hold such nonsense has had upon the human mind is historical, anthropological, and psychological. The elect, of course, are ourselves, the damned, our enemies or those we disapprove of: egoism, self-assertion and aggression are dominant human characteristics. Such teachings appeal to them, support them, and minister to them.

Arnold renewed his attack here on Dissent, on religious grounds: he characterized it as irreligious, if it were not so ludicrous – we must remember how much to the fore it was in his time, and the harm it had wrought since the seventeenth century. (How much Swift would have agreed!) 'Is it not, as to discipline, that his [the Puritan's] self-importance is fomented by the fuss, bustle, and partisanship of a private sect, instead of being lost in the greatness of a public body? As to worship, is it not that his taste is pleased by usages and words that come down to *him*, instead of drawing him up to them? by services which reflect, instead of the culture of great men, the crude culture of himself and his fellows? And as to doctrine, is it not that his mind is pleased at hearing no opinion but his own?'

Enough of the diagnosis. Arnold's constructive argument was for comprehension in a national church, a national society for the promotion of goodness. This had been Dr Arnold's ideal, but in his day the erosion of belief in doctrine had gone nothing like so far. The paradox is that not until the sects had ceased to believe in their doctrinal nonsense was any measure of ecumenism possible. Matthew Arnold's problem was to reduce the doctrinal nonsense (in contrast to a C. S. Lewis in our time) so as to salvage as much good as was credible to a rational person in that age. The objective problem became – how much of recognizable, historic Christianity was left?

Arnold conceived of himself as defending the heart of Christianity at a time when the working class, as well as others, were ceasing to believe in its supernatural claims, in miracles, or in the Bible. He was much disturbed at this, as well he might be: he saw that it did not do for simple people to lose the faith they had lived by, either for themselves or for society. Religion had kept them on the rails. Now they were ceasing to believe in it. What was to be done?

There was a further crux which he hardly faced. Since the mass of mankind were so simple and foolish, might it not be that the simple nonsense of faith suited their simplicity better? Anyone who has observed the effectiveness of the cults at work in Catholic churches – the faithful with hands upon a fetich of the Sacred Heart in St Patrick's Cathedral in New York, let alone more primitive anthropological observances which even the Archbishop of Lisbon has been unable to suppress in Portugal, such as licking the sacred steps in Holy Week until they run with blood – will realize that the view of human nature endorsed by the Catholic Church is more in accordance with it than that of the more rational Protestant sects. Arnold was right to hold that they were doomed and that there was more of a future for Catholicism, founded upon the rock of the irrational.

He wanted Catholicism, too, to rid itself of its excrescences, its Ultramontanism, everything that Manning stood for. Arnold was sympathetic to Newman, cited his view of the development of doctrine, and the overwhelming impression that the claim of the Roman Church to be universal had had upon him: *Securus judicat orbis terrarum* settled the question. But in his *Essay on the Development of Christian Doctrine* Newman had framed the question to suggest the answer. Considering the past two thousand years only, and restricting oneself to Western Europe, then the Roman Church occupied the centre of the picture. But historically the prominence of Christianity in the world simply reflected the ascendancy of Europe in the world of the nineteenth century. In the wider perspective of today China bulks largest, with one-quarter of the human race and its future largely dependent upon it; but besides the Far East, with Indo-China, Japan, India, there is emergent Africa; there is the Moslem world, and the Communist world, to go no further. The universal claims of Christianity are not what they were, nor its relevance to the modern world.

Arnold's point of departure was, once more, the kindred spirit of Renan, who had declared in his book on St Paul, 'after having been, for three hundred years, thanks to Protestantism, the Christian doctor *par excellence*, Paul is now coming to the end of his reign.' Arnold was much more sympathetic to this uncongenial spirit, and set about re-interpreting him in a modernist sense, arguing that he had been misinterpreted by Protestantism in far too rigorous a sense. We need not go into the argument; for, when Arnold urges that Paul's mental world was so remote from our own, with his Judaic concepts of nearly two thousand years ago, that there was no knowing now what precisely he meant, the same point applies to Arnold's attempt to make sense of what he thought. The core of Arnold's critique is the attempt to get behind all the argumentation of the Epistle to the Romans, which has had such an appalling influence in the Protestant tradition, to drop doctrine and external observances, for the inner life of the spirit. Arnold had no hesitation in interpreting St Paul's justification by faith (which had caused so much misery over the centuries) to mean simply, 'a holding fast to an unseen power of goodness, identification with Christ'.

With no belief in a personal God, Arnold was induced to put forward the view that the universe was moved, or at least motivated, by 'a stream of tendency making for goodness'; and that true religion was an inner disposition to put oneself into relation, and as far as possible into accord, with that. What is most revealing of him personally is a moving passage on the power of love, which he put forward by analogy with the religious spirit: 'Of such a mysterious power and its operation some clear notion may be got by anybody who has ever had any overpowering attachment, or has been in love. Everyone knows how being in love changes for the time a man's spiritual atmosphere, and makes animation and buoyancy where before there was flatness and dullness. One may even say that this is the reason why being in love is so popular with the whole human race – because it relieves in so irresistible and delightful a manner the tedium or depression of commonplace human life.'

Herbert Paul, who knew Arnold, regarded *Literature and Dogma* (1873) as marking 'a distinct and definite epoch' of his life: 'with this book he severed himself from orthodox Christianity, and even from Unitarianism. He had indeed a curious dislike of Unitarians, which he may have inherited from his father' – he probably regarded them as even bleaker than other Nonconformists. 'Yet his own creed, if creed it can be called, would have horrified Dr Arnold far more than theirs.' This year his mother died, so he was free from that benevolent shadow, and could speak out: 'For he rejected not merely miracles, but the personality of God.' The Doctor, we have seen, was peculiarly penetrated by the thought of God, through and through, almost every moment of the day. Rugby Chapel was a monument to his personal sense of a personal God, with whom he was on intimate terms – the Headmaster of the universe. Nor did his son 'always express himself in reverent language, and with a due regard for the feelings of others'. He was persuaded to omit a passage in which he had compared a confused, well-meaning person, of some eminence at the time, to the confusing mystery of the Trinity.

This calls attention to an aspect of Arnold apt to be overlooked. He is given so much credit for urbanity, gentlemanly good manners in controversy, that it is surprising what things he did say – things we should hardly dare to utter. More important, how brave it was of him to utter them, in the inspissated atmosphere of Victorian religiosity, the unspoken censorship riveted upon people's minds in such matters, the tabus erected to protect nonsense beliefs! Arnold made no bones about what he thought in an age when Bishop Wilberforce, Soapy Sam, was an archetypal figure.

Arnold conceived of himself as performing a positive service for Christianity, reducing it to the essence of Christ's message, freed from the doctrinal trash which people were ceasing to believe anyway. On one flank he had the militant rationalists, ranged behind the leading philosopher of the age, John Stuart Mill, who were complete unbelievers, hostile to Christianity and the churches; these included Arnold's own friend Huxley, and atheists like Bradlaugh and Clifford who gave a lead to the Radical tradition of unbelief among working-people. Arnold saw no good in that – and here he was right enough. On the other side were the embattled churches in possession of the field, with the weight of Victorian society behind.

Between these two it was a lonely battle that he waged. But he was, except for his family – and perhaps even there – an essentially lonely man. To this he owed his originality, his freedom from the conventional views that dogged others. Only half an Englishman, though unconscious of this, he was at heart an outsider. This freed him – and it is extraordinary how forward-looking he was in religion, quite as much as in the field of education. With the reduction of dogma and doctrinal beliefs, the Christian churches have been able to come together to do good work, as never before. *This* was what he was looking forward to.

He was often attacked for vagueness, because he would not sub-scribe to doctrines. But he was perfectly clear in his own mind as to what Christ's message meant – the kingdom of God is within you, seek to follow God's will, not your own, etc. Arnold held that it meant self-control, self-renouncement, an end to selfishness; love for others, consideration for their well-being, as much as one's own; only this gives happiness and joy in life. What is more, he followed the prescription in his own life – and, like Eliot, his most eminent disciple in our time, he found that it worked. So he had inner security to support him in his brave battle for sense in these matters.

He was constantly taunted with being no metaphysician – which he was not. He turned this aside by saying that metaphysics in this realm was no help, only created difficulties for people: 'All these fancies come from an excessive turn for reasoning, and from a neglect of observing men's actual course of thinking and way of using words.' It is ironical that the metaphysicians themselves today have come round to Arnold's way of thinking. Such a symptomatic book as Ryle's *Concept of Mind*, indeed the whole inflexion of philosophy today – with its abnegation of metaphysical claims, and its modest examination of actual usage and meaning – is far more in keeping with Arnold's way of thought than the schools of philosophy that dominated his own time. He saved time and energy by disregarding them, leaving them to their own specialisms.

'Far more of our mistakes come from want of fresh knowledge than from want of correct reasoning; and therefore letters meet a greater want in us than does logic.' This is not to deny logic its proper place, of specific but limited utility and narrow application. But how often following narrow chains of logical reasoning led men to make mistakes. Newman had his own remedy for this in his 'illative sense', put forward in his last, most original work, *An Essay in Aid of a Grammar of Assent*, at this time (1870) – no doubt Arnold read it. He considered that 'a wide and familiar acquaintance with the human spirit and its productions, showing how ideas and terms arose, and what is their character', offered a better guide. 'And this is letters and history, not logic. So that minds with small aptitude for abstruse reasoning may yet, through letters, gain some hold on sound judgment and useful knowledge, and may even clear up blunders committed, out of their very excess of talent, by the athletes of logic.'

How pertinent this warning was we may see from the appalling example of a Bertrand Russell in our time, whose whole life was a career of such blunders, both private and public, some of the most dangerous character – as when he advocated dropping a nuclear bomb on Moscow. Fancy taking such a person for a guide, moral or political![1] He should have confined himself to logic, where he was a specialist.

We need not therefore – indeed we must not – follow Arnold into the details of his dusty combats with obtuse adversaries, simply emphasize his own large aim: to disentangle and clarify 'the natural truth of Christianity'. (He would have been on even stronger ground if he had made his regular phrase 'the natural truth, or truths, *in* Christianity'.) He was so anxious to preserve the best in it – rightly, against the militant rationalists, who would throw it away; and as

---

[1] cf. Michael Foot on Russell: 'he is my man of the century'!

against the orthodox who were ceasing to carry conviction, even among themselves. Newman fell back on faith, where he was inexpugnable and could not be touched by reason – and believed in the miracle of the liquefaction of the blood of St Januarius, as the idiot populace of Naples did. All this, to Arnold, offered no hope, and was 'frankly impossible'.

A comparable idiocy Arnold had to contend with, far more widespread in nineteenth-century England and America, was belief in the literal inspiration of the Bible, written by the hand of God, every word of it. Even Newman had written, 'the Bible is the record of the whole revealed faith; so far all parties agree.' No one dared to say that it was just the record of the experience and beliefs of the Jews, that it was just history, ethics, law and poetry, no magic talisman by which other peoples and experiences, later in time and more advanced in civilization, were to be judged. For the English-speaking peoples Bishop Colenso had begun the process of eliciting the sense of the Old Testament, primitive and barbarous in many respects, in his epoch-making work on the Pentateuch. Arnold had been notoriously unfair to Colenso, for reasons rather difficult to clarify – I think he objected mainly to Colenso's simplicity of approach (he was a mathematician, who showed what nonsense Old Testament statistics were), his lack of sophistication (he was a Cambridge man), and his disregard of expediency (he was a Cornishman). All that Colenso cared for was the truth. Arnold would not go so far as to place the *Book of Genesis* on a par with Hesiod's *Theogony*, which is its proper place.

The New Testament offered a greater challenge to popular beliefs, and what was more in question was when it came to the truth of Christian claims. Here Arnold can be described summarily as a Modernist. No biblical expert (he learned Hebrew and consulted his Jewish friends), he argued sensibly that one could not expect Jesus always to have been correctly reported by his reporters (Arnold's own experience with the press brought this home to him), and the early Christian hopes as to a Second Coming, shared by Jesus himself, were obviously mistaken.

He thought that it was a mistake for Christianity to attach itself to nonsense beliefs – it should concentrate on the essence of its message.

From this point of view 'the Protestant notion is doomed to an earlier ruin than the Catholic'. This was a brave thing to say in Victorian England, hag-ridden with Protestant sectaries; and it would have infuriated Dr Arnold, who thought the exact opposite – and was wrong. The Doctor had written, in favour of Catholic Emancipation, that once it was granted, Protestantism would make its way in Ireland!

So much for the obtuseness of Matt's father. What Matt himself hoped for appears in a letter to his French pastor friend, diagnosing that the sectarian narrowness of French Protestantism would be their end as 'a religious organisation, as it will be fatal to Protestant Dissent in this country. My ideal would be, for Catholic countries, the development of something like Old Catholicism, retaining as much as possible of old religious services and usages, but becoming more and more liberal in spirit. And your Protestant Church I should like to see disposing itself to meet half-way a Catholic movement of this kind, and to ally itself with it.' He did not say that the Church of England historically, perhaps providentially, represented something of the sort: an authentic *via media*. We see him uncomfortably poised, somewhere between Manning and Moody, and as usual it is the sensible man in the middle of the road who receives most brickbats.

Arnold replied to his numerous critics in *God and the Bible: A Review of Objections to 'Literature and Dogma'*. In England, where the orthodox held all the strongholds, his book had aroused alarm. Not so in New England, as we have seen, where the Unitarians and Congregationalists ruled opinion: they did him the justice to recognize that his aim was to preserve as much as was possible of Christianity. Opinion on the Continent regarded his book as conservative. The lead in biblical scholarship and criticism had now passed to the German universities. Arnold acquainted himself with their work and appreciated its value, without subscribing to their more fanciful theorizing. He retained the common-sense and experienced judgment of a man of letters, which was what he had to guide him in these unrewarding wastes of theologizing. A good classical scholar who could read German – which was more than Newman could – he was quite sufficiently equipped to criticize and make sense of the documents of early Christianity. He conscientiously read them up.

'As our traditional theology breaks up, German criticism of the Bible is likely to be studied here more and more.' He insisted that his aim was not destructive: 'I have always thought, therefore, that merely to destroy the illusions of popular Christianity was indefensible.' It may be this that accounts for his renewed injustice to Bishop Colenso – or perhaps he had a bad conscience about him: 'Dr Colenso had nothing, and hence our dissatisfaction with his work.' But what about truth? Colenso was as much concerned to establish what was sensible and true in the Old Testament – a stumbling block to missionary work among blacks – as Arnold was for the New Testament. Colenso was a simple, believing Christian, who suffered far more for his pursuit of truth than Arnold ever did. And Colenso was a leading biblical scholar, well acquainted with Continental work, who proceeded step by step with the findings of Kuenen to make his own contribution in this field. His work created the greatest uproar of the kind of the century, except for that over Darwin; Colenso was monstrously vilified and persecuted, but he was the pioneer of the Higher Criticism in Britain. Arnold was unjust to his work.

His view was that men could not do with Victorian Christianity as it was, yet they could not do without it; he rather overlooked the possibilities of their doing without it. He asked the reason for 'the astonishing popularity of the American revivalists', such people as Moody and Sankey – and gave too rational an answer. It needed no other explanation than the usual idiocy of the masses – the kind of thing the ancient philosopher Celsus had objected to in the early Christians: he could not take them seriously intellectually. Arnold wanted to get down to what could be so taken: 'The first Christians misunderstood Jesus and had the multitude's appetite for miracles, the multitude's inexact observation and boundless credulity.' There was no point in taking *them* as evidence.

On the other hand, what revolutionary rationalists – Proudhon and Michelet, he might have added Marx and Engels, if he had known of them – had to offer was no substitute: 'It is much more surprising that they should ever have reckoned that their ideas of revolution and liberty, and the spread of physical science dispelling a host of illusions, could at all do for the world what Christianity had done for it and serve as a substitute for Christianity.' Hence, for example, the spiritual desert that is Russia under Communism, as Solzhenitsyn grieves. What has Marxism to offer, compared with 'the necessity of Christianity, its power and charm for the heart, mind, and imagination of man?' And this, 'even though the preternatural, which is now its popular sanction, should have to be given up. To show this was the end for which both books were written.'

Arnold ended with a defence of his father, who had been attacked for knowing no theology. 'But Dr Arnold, who had a sound historical instinct', wrote his son, 'could tell at once from the warnings of this instinct that theology, which is a series of conclusions upon the history in the Bible, had apprehended that history all wrong; that it was faulty therefore in its very base, and so could not be a true theology, a science of the Christian religion, at all.' This episode must have given Arnold the comforting feeling that he had his father with him after all, and that the son was carrying forward his father's work.

Two years later, in 1877, he published *Last Essays on Church and Religion*, his final work on these subjects: 'Indirectly such questions must often in all serious literary work, present themselves; but in this volume I make them my direct object for the last time.' He lets us know what had impelled him into this field: 'I became engaged in it against my will, from being led by particular circumstances to remark the deteriorating effect of the temper and strifes of Dissent upon good men, the lamentable waste of power and usefulness which was thereby caused.' It was obvious to him that 'the old anthropomorphic and miraculous religion no longer reaches and rules as it once did.' He was most of all disturbed by religion failing to appeal to the working classes, except in its grossest and most materializing forms. 'And it is to be remedied by a gradual transformation of the popular mind, by slowly curing it of its grossness of perception and of its materialising habits, not by keeping religion materialistic that it may correspond to them.' In the educational field he had devoted a life's work to that end; here, then, was another side to that endeavour.

He realized how provincial the upholders of orthodoxy were in England, how much out of touch with opinion on the Continent, where 'the whole force of progressive and liberal opinion has pronounced against the Christian religion.' Here, consistently, was another reason for his attack on the self-satisfaction of the Victorian English. The real question was whether the liberal rejection of Christianity was to be accepted, or whether it could stand by maintaining the best in itself.

Arnold was not at all vague as to what this meant in the realm of conduct, which he said, metaphorically, made up three-fourths of life. It was a matter of experience that 'the only real happiness is in a kind of impersonal higher life, where the happiness of others counts with a man as essential to his own. He that loves his life does really turn out to lose it, and the new commandment proves its own truth by experience.' The new commandment was that of Jesus: 'Jesus Christ and his precepts are found to hit the moral experience of mankind, to hit it in the critical points, to hit it lastingly. . . . So that of the two great Christian virtues, charity and chastity – kindness and pureness – the one has at this moment the most signal testimony from experience to its intrinsic truth and weight, the other is expecting it.'

There is no doubt that this is what Arnold had himself experienced, and used for rule of life in the sorrows that hit him hard in these very years, with the deaths of the three sons he loved. Underneath the urbane exterior there was an exceedingly tender heart. One is reminded of the simple words of the most brilliant mind of the Northern Renaissance: on his deathbed Erasmus relapsed into his childhood tongue to say, 'Love God'. Arnold had much in common with him.

Invited to address the London clergy, he put forward his view of the Church of England in unclerical terms, which derived from Dr Arnold, as a 'great national institution for the promotion of goodness'. This enabled him to outflank the gathering campaign in the Liberal Party for its disestablishment. John Morley urged in the *Fortnightly Review* that this was 'a question which the very Spirit of Time has borne on into the first place . . . The Church of England is the ally of tyranny, the organ of social oppression, the champion of intellectual bondage.' This was Liberal humbug, but it rallied the Nonconformists behind the Party.

Arnold was more concerned at 'the estrangement of the working classes', and he was careful to dissociate the Church from any necessary dependence on the existing class-system: 'Certainly the superstitious worship of existing social facts, a devoted obsequiousness to the landed and propertied and satisfied classes, does not inhere in the Christian religion.' Nevertheless, the essence of Christ's gospel was not to be found in the mistaken expectations by his followers of a Second Coming in triumph to rule on earth, but in the inner kingdom of the spirit: 'This was the ideal of Jesus: the establishment on earth of God's kingdom, of felicity, not by the violent processes of our Fifth Monarchy men, or of the German Anabaptists, or of the French Communists, but by the establishment on earth of God's righteousness.'

And so Arnold took his leave: 'The thing which I proposed to myself to do has, so far as my powers enabled me to do it, been done. What I wished to say has been said. And in returning to devote to literature, more strictly so-called, what remains to me of life and strength and leisure, I am returning, after all, to a field where work of the most important kind has now to be done, though indirectly, for religion. I am persuaded that the transformation of religion, which is essential for its perpetuance, can be accomplished only by carrying the qualities of flexibility, perceptiveness and judgment, which are the best fruits of letters, to whole classes of the community which now know nothing of them, and by procuring the application of those qualities to matters where they are never applied now.'

There was reproach in that last phrase; but here was a double justification for his double campaign. Literature and religion were not divorced from each other, and each could perform a service to the other.

The essay, 'Bishop Butler and the Zeit-Geist' (i.e. Spirit of the Time), shows Arnold's mind moving back from these religious concerns to

175

literature. He was not an historian, unlike his father; but, for a poet and literary man, he was sympathetic to the historical approach and appreciated how important it was, for a correct estimate, to view the subject in the conditions determining his work. This is his leading theme with the philosopher Butler, of whom he gives an appealing biographical sketch – would that he had done more of that kind of thing. Even Butler, with all his originality, was constricted by the historic circumstances of time and place, the eighteenth-century Church. Hence his handling of 'miracles and prophecy is not in proportion to his great powers of mind. Butler could not well, indeed, have then handled miracles and prophecy satisfactorily; the time was not ripe for it. Men's knowledge increases, their point of view changes, they come to see things differently.' This is the historical approach *par excellence*.

Butler exerted a marked influence upon the elect minds of the nineteenth century, in particular, Newman and Gladstone. Arnold, for all his admiration for Butler, was curiously captious about the *Analogy*. He thought it a failure. It had, however, said all that could be said for religious belief, from the point of view of eighteenth-century reason. What was original was that Butler gave it a psychological basis, grounded it in human nature. Christian beliefs 'in themselves entirely fall in with our natural sense of things'; further, the tendency of good to win through pointed to 'somewhat moral in the constitution of things'; further still, and perhaps in consequence, 'our happiness and misery *are* trusted to our conduct, and made to depend upon it.' Butler could not offer more than probability; but he was a reasonable man, as well as a psychologist. Arnold does not seem to have been drawn to psychology. At the end he offers a comment which is a pointer to himself: 'The power of religion which actuated him was, as is the case with so many of us, better, profounder, and happier, than the scheme of religion which he could draw out in his books.'

There is an increasingly historical interest in his later literary essays. 'Falkland' dealt with another kindred spirit: Arnold evidently saw him as a precursor, a moderate middle-of-the-road man, unhappy with either side in the full bloom of political and religious party-spirit. Arnold quotes Clarendon – with a sniff at his elaborate reverberating, splendid style: Falkland 'had in his own judgment such a latitude in opinion that he did not believe any part of the order or government of it to be so essentially necessary to religion but that it might be parted with, and altered for a notable benefit or convenience.'

Evidently a seventeenth-century Arnold – and it did not commend him any the less that the Nonconformists, descendants of the Puritans, did not hold with his commemoration. Falkland found both sides in the Civil War at fault – as they were: 'the cause of neither was sound. Falkland had lucidity enough to see it. This is what makes his figure and situation so truly tragic.' Arnold's conclusion was that it was not the popular party-man, John Hampden, who was the true martyr: 'If we are to find a martyr in the history of the Great Civil War, let it be Falkland. He was the martyr of lucidity of mind and largeness of temper, in a strife of imperfect intelligences and tempers illiberal.' This is a judgment to which the non-party historian can subscribe.

And what of the greatest genius among the Puritans, John Milton?

In the last months of his life Arnold gave an address at the unveiling of a window in Milton's memory, given by an American, in St Margaret's Westminster – the House of Commons church, because they would not attend service in the Abbey with its 'copes and wafers'. Arnold began with a comment on the cult of the 'average man' in America: 'the *average man* is too much a religion there; his performance is unduly magnified, his shortcomings are not duly seen and admitted.' Since then, the average man has won out everywhere – with consequences for civilization and culture that Arnold would have detested.

To what did Milton owe his 'supreme distinction'? – 'To nature first and foremost, to that bent of nature for inequality which to the worshippers of the average man is so unacceptable.' Nevertheless, natural distinction and inequality of gifts are facts of life; 'and when the right standard of excellence is lost, it is not likely that much which is excellent will be produced'.

Arnold's literary criticism was not divorced, in any obtuse or sterile way, from his social criticism, from history and society.

He had devoted a fuller essay to his French friend Edmond Scherer's book on Milton. He began with an onslaught on Macaulay, so representative a Victorian, who expressed much that Arnold disliked in his age – its brash self-complacency, its unsubtle overconfidence, its rhetoric and partisanship. Macaulay's essay on Milton had brought him fame overnight. I do not know that Arnold resented this, but one can only say that fame was very easily won in that small, literate society. Arnold had already disparaged Macaulay's celebrated style – so effective with the public, so rhetorical with its parliamentary antitheses, so clamorous and clanging, ultimately vulgar. Now it was Macaulay's unsoundness: 'the writer has not for his aim to see and to utter the real truth about his object. . . . A right understanding did not "spontaneously issue" in the mind of Macaulay, because Macaulay's mind was that of a rhetorician, not of a disinterested critic.'

What was Milton really like, when one looked into the object? Arnold quoted Milton at work, on an opponent of his tract on Divorce: 'how should he, a serving man both by nature and function, an idiot by breeding, and a solicitor by presumption, ever come to know or to feel within himself what the meaning is of *gentle?*' Arnold was a gentleman, and objected to such language; but had he not said equally nasty things about the Nonconformists, and called the Reverend Ward Beecher – brother of the argumentative Mrs Beecher Stowe – a 'heated barbarian'?

The point that arises in literary or historical controversy is – what terms are fitting for which persons. If one is dealing with a subtle and polite opponent who understands the point at issue, one should deal with him politely and subtly. If one has an obtuse fool, who does not know what he is talking about – say, about Shakespeare in terms of his age – then it is a duty to tell him that he does not know what he is talking about. One should devote no time to crackpots who think that Shakespeare wrote the works of Bacon, or that Sir Thomas More killed the Princes in the Tower. On this point, my sympathies are with Milton, who reacted to third-rate critics of his work with –

I did but prompt the age to quit their clogs
  By the known rules of ancient liberty,
  When straight a barbarous noise environs me
  Of owls and cuckoos, asses, apes and dogs . . .
  But this is got by casting pearl to hogs
  That bawl for freedom in their senseless mood,
    And still revolt when Truth would set them free.

Surprisingly, Arnold was unappreciative of *Paradise Lost.* He thought the subject hardly suitable for an epic; 'it is really a commentary on a Biblical text, the first two or three chapters of Genesis.' Its effect depended 'upon our being able to take it literally. Merely as matter of poetry, the story of the Fall has no special force or effectiveness; its effectiveness for us comes, and can only come, from our taking it all as the literal narrative of what positively happened.' Arnold reserved his enthusiasm for Milton's style: 'Alone of English poets, alone in English art, Milton has it: he is our great artist in style, our one first-rate master in the grand style. He is as truly a master in this style as the great Greeks are, or Virgil, or Dante.' Arnold related this to the moral elevation of Milton's mind – nor is that in the least lessened by his contempt for the third-rate.

We must not traverse the whole of Arnold's later criticism – there is not much of it – merely bring out what is personal and revealing of the man. A second series of *Essays in Criticism* was brought together in the year after his death, by 'C.' – presumably Lord Coleridge. The essay on Wordsworth has the added interest that Arnold had known him well. Wordsworth had never been a popular poet, had been constantly depreciated, and Arnold found that interest in him, such as it had been, was now declining: 'To tenth-rate critics and compilers . . . it is still permissible to speak of Wordsworth's poetry not only with ignorance, but with impertinence. On the Continent he is almost unknown.'

Arnold himself did most to remedy this state of affairs. His admirable selection of the best in Wordsworth succeeded with the public, and his Preface placed him third among English poets, after only Shakespeare and Milton. It is doubtful if ranging the poets in this manner has any use – the essential thing is to observe their differences and individual qualities. The question is one of recognition, and the ability to recognize quality – ordinary people can never tell unless they are told. Arnold told them.

He felt a kinship not only with Wordsworth but also with Gray. Except for the 'Elegy', Gray was again not a popular poet: 'Gray's poetry, on the whole, astonished his contemporaries at first more than it pleased them: it was so unfamiliar, so unlike the sort of poetry in vogue.' Arnold brought out, what was not realized by the public, the extraordinary range of scholarship of the author of the 'Elegy in a Country Churchyard'; and also, hardly less surprising, that Gray was most himself when writing humorously. Horace Walpole said that 'humour was his natural and original turn'. But he was a lonely spirit, with extraordinary qualities of mind: 'Maintaining and fortifying them by lofty studies, he yet could not fully educe and enjoy them; the want of a genial atmosphere, the failure of sympathy in his contemporaries, were too great.' This must have said something for Arnold too.

In his essay, 'The Study of Poetry', he spoke out in no uncertain terms. He quoted himself – it is true that repetition is a 'besetting sin' of Arnold's prose: 'there is not a creed which is not shaken, not an accredited dogma which is not shown to be questionable, not a received tradition which does not threaten to dissolve.' Only poetry remains, only art transcends time. The ultimate critical judgment of literature and art is an aesthetic one, neither historical nor personal. The historical judgment is liable to bias in favour of the past, 'the personal estimate when we are dealing with poets who are our contemporaries, or at any rate modern'. Though Arnold did not say so, the latter leads to greater distortion: he himself was unfair to Tennyson, his friend Sainte-Beuve was incapable of justice towards his contemporaries, Victor Hugo, Balzac, Baudelaire, Flaubert. On the other hand, historical sense was a preservative against the erection of a static classicism as the standard to be imposed for all art – as with eighteenth-century painting and seventeenth- and eighteenth-century French poetry: 'Above all, for the historian this is inadmissible; for it withdraws the poet from his time, from his proper life, it breaks historical relationships, it blinds criticism by conventional admiration, and renders the investigation of literary origins unacceptable.'

He says in salutary fashion that the value of negative criticism lies only in that it clears the way for positive appreciation. One sees what contempt he would have for the querulous, personally motivated criticism so rife today, in a literary world that reflects the decline of standards in society at large. Arnold's standards were extraordinarily exacting, possibly too much so, certainly for comfort. We see this at work in what he says of Chaucer – who might well challenge the place Arnold had allotted to Wordsworth: 'Of Chaucer's divine liquidness of diction, his divine fluidity of movement, it is difficult to speak temperately.' Such enthusiasm is rare with Arnold. 'And yet something is wanting to the poetry of Chaucer, which poetry must have before it can be placed in the glorious class of the best.' What was wanting was the quality Aristotle demanded, 'high seriousness'.

'Critics give themselves great labour to draw out what in the abstract constitutes the characters of a high quality of poetry.' Arnold refused to go into abstract critical analysis: he thought it pointless. 'It is much better simply to have recourse to concrete examples: to take specimens of poetry of the high, the very highest quality, and to say – the characters of a high quality of poetry are what is expressed *there*. They are far better recognized by being felt in the verse of the master, than by being perused in the prose of the critic.'

This is the conclusion of a foremost practising poet and the first critic of his time. It has its pointed application today when criticism is made an end in itself by third-rate minds (*he* called them tenth-rate), and the appreciation of literature, which is the purpose of criticism, is obstructed by the conceits and concepts of analysis, whether of meaning or ambiguity: a sterile scholasticism moving further and further away from literature, with its fundamental concern with the human.

CHAPTER 9

The Family and the Man

IT IS SAD that in the last three decades of his life Arnold kept hoping against hope that he might return to poetry. In 1861 he was writing to his mother, 'I must finish off for the present my critical writings between this and fifty, and give the next ten years earnestly to poetry. It is my last chance. It is not a bad ten years of one's life for poetry if one resolutely uses it, but it is a time in which, if one does not use it, one dries up and becomes prosaic altogether.' Two years later it is, 'after the summer I mean to lie fallow again for some time, or to busy myself with poetry only'. Twenty years later, within two years of the end: 'I wonder if I shall ever get anything more done in poetry.' To the very end he kept hoping that he might finish his verse-drama 'Lucretius', which was to crown his achievement. He might have done if he had lived longer: he was only sixty-five when he died.

During these years to within fifteen of his end, his mother kept the light burning at Fox How for all the family; she, and her daughter Jane Forster, were Matt's real confidantes, who understood his aims and hopes best. He was determined that there should be no biography of him, and instructed that his letters to 'K' about his poems be destroyed: they were thought in the family to contain the secret of Marguerite. He must have himself destroyed his mother's letters to him, for some of hers to his brother Tom remain. When his own fascinating letters were published, his widow cut out most intimate references to herself; his emotional life was singularly concentrated within his family, so an element of warmth has been lost in the usual public picture of him.

Tom's daughter, Mrs Humphry Ward, had a very clear memory of the old lady of Fox How. 'Her beautiful hair was scarcely touched with grey, her complexion was still delicately clear, and her soft brown eyes had the eager sympathetic look of her Cornish race.' The dominant impression she gave was one of gentleness and charm; but she was a woman of character and intuitive tact, who guided her family of remarkable children, with marked individualities, to the best purpose: she was their lode-star. 'Matthew Arnold adored her, and wrote to her every week of his life' – what a pity that we have not her letters back to him!

Her grand-daughter says that there was 'something ardent and responsive in her temperament, that attracted able men' to repose their confidences in her; her intelligence was quick, her sympathies wide, but it was her judgment, above all, that commanded Dean Stanley's admiration. Clough was particularly devoted to her, for it was she who made him a member of the family at Rugby, with his own parents absent in America. This must have counted for something in Matt's special feeling for him, when they were so different. When *The Bothie* came out, she wrote with kindly tact, 'the poem is as remarkable, I think, as you would expect coming from him. Its *power* quite overcame my dislike to the measure – so far at least as to make me read it with great interest.' There we have her, sympathetic and tactful – and she was quite right as to the measure. Then – she is writing to Tom in New Zealand, on a Sunday in November: 'now the others have gone off to Rydal Chapel without me this lovely Sunday morning. There are the bells sounding invitingly across the valley, and the evergreens are white and sparkling in the sun.' We see that she had her own poetry.

She had been responsible, we remember, for the step, the secretary-ship to Lord Lansdowne, that led to Matt's career in life. When she made a rare visit to London he visited her practically every day, 'so unspoiled by his being so much sought after in a kind of society entirely different from anything we can enter into'. From the grandeur of Lansdowne House Matt wrote to Tom in the Antipodes, when they were young and life was all before them – with its griefs for Matt and its futility for Tom: 'Here I sit, opposite a marble group of Romulus and Remus and the wolf. Above it is a great picture, Rembrandt's Jewish Exiles, which would do for Consuelo and

Albert resting in one of their wanderings worn out upon a wild stony heath.' We recall his passionate devotion to George Sand, which had led him to make his pilgrimage to Nohant.

'Behind me a most musical clock, marking now 24 minutes past 1 p.m. On my left two great windows looking out on the court in front of the house, through one of which comes in gushes the soft damp breath, with a tone of spring life in it, which the close of an English February brings. The green lawn which occupies nearly half the court is studded over with crocuses of all colours – growing out of the grass. And from the square and the neighbouring streets, through the open door whereat the civil porter moves to and fro, come the sounds of vehicles and men, some from near and some from far, but mellowed by the time they reach this backstanding lordly mansion. But above all cries comes one whereat every stone in this and other lordly mansions may totter and quake for fear:

"Se . . . c . . . ond Edition of the Morning Herald – L . . . a . . . test news from Paris – Arrival of the King of the French." '

It is the February Revolution of 1848, with Clough full of ardent expectation in Paris, and Matt himself moved. What a marvellous evocation of the moment, the place, the scene! And now it has all vanished – or, rather, been destroyed, everything dispersed.

And here is Matt at home at Fox How, drawn by his mother: 'Matt has been very much pleased, I think, by what he has seen of dear old Wordsworth since he has been at home, and certainly he manages to draw him out well. The old man was here yesterday, and as he sat on the stool in the corner by the fire which you [Tom] knew so well, he talked of various subjects of interest, of Italian poetry, of Coleridge, etc.; and he looked and spoke with more vigour than he has often done lately.' Shortly he was on his death-bed; as Matt's sisters walked in the April sun along the mountain side, they looked across at the old house, where unseen hands drew down the blinds.

The years 1868 to 1872 bore hardly upon Matt and his wife: three of their four sons died. First, his child Basil. Matt wrote to his mother, 'this morning he was photographed – we should else have had no picture of him whatever; and now he lies in his little grey coffin, with his hands folded on his breast, and a little cross of double white prim-roses placed in them, looking sweeter and more touching than I can say.' They buried him at Laleham, where all this family life began with the Doctor's happy marriage to Mary Penrose.

At the end of this year there was a second blow, with the death of Tommy, at sixteen, at Harrow. The boy had always been delicate and unable to take to schooling normally; so his parents moved house to Harrow to look after him, though he was only there for a term. He could not take part in the games, or in the work much; his talent was for music. He composed in his head, but it was not until his last illness that he wrote down a setting of Lord Houghton's children's poem, 'Good Night and Good Morning', which became quite well known. The little work was published, with coloured etchings by Walter Severn, the son of Keats's friend. Arnold wrote to Lord Houghton:

> I send you, as I promised, my poor Tommy's setting of your pretty words in which he took great delight. He composed a great deal but wrote hardly anything down; it luckily happened that during his illness he noted down with his shaky little fingers the music for these words of yours, and we have just this one thing to remind us of his talent for music, which was a very genuine one. The melody is quite simple, but musicians tell me they are struck with its natural correctness and grace, and with its being so wholly untouched by the depression of his illness. The words are charming.

This musical strain was quite unlike the Arnolds, who had no ear. As we have seen, it appeared again in a younger son, Richard Pen-rose, who showed early promise in composition, which came to nothing, except for his companionship with Elgar, who used to play over *his* compositions with him.

It is from this year of grief, 1868, that Arnold's private Note-Books gather momentum and record more and more fully the reading that spoke to his spirit, so that we can follow in them – unknown to his time – his spiritual pilgrimage. He was a most conscientious reading man – perhaps too much so for a poet; but in his arduous journeyings about the country he filled up the crevices and *longueurs* with reading, and in six languages – his quotations are always in the original, mostly Greek and Latin, French and German, besides English.

Reading provided the company this essentially lonely, though outwardly sociable, man kept: 'The importance of reading, not slight stuff to get through the time, but the best that has been written, forces itself upon me more and more every year I live. It is living in good company, the best company, and people are generally quite keen, or too keen, about doing that; yet they will not do it in the simplest and most innocent manner by reading.' This was written to a sister; but he had already preached as much to the public in *Culture and Anarchy*: 'how much a man's life of each day depends for its solidity and value on whether he reads during *that* day and, far more still, on what he reads during it.'

The admirable editors of the Note-Books tell us that he read wherever he was, 'in the British Museum, at the Athenaeum, in continental hotels, on railway trains, at home, and even in America'. There is actually a comment on Karl Marx, but from an article on him; for few were the Victorian English who were aware of the existence in their midst of the man who was to overthrow their world. The quotation says, 'society is a sort of organism on the growth of which conscious efforts can exercise little effect.' Several such entries reveal Arnold's depressing conviction that he could see little change for all his life of effort. Yet numerous entries show him spurring himself on to do his duty day by day, in spite of all discouragements. He did not see the reward of his labours, far greater than with any contemporary writer – except Karl Marx: their respective rewards came in this century.

From early on, in more fragmentary jottings in the 1850s, we watch him disciplining himself to his work. *Ein unnütz Leben ist ein früher Tod* (Goethe): an unuseful life is an early death. Again and again he quotes, *Semper aliquid certi proponendum est*, from the *Imitation of Christ* of Thomas à Kempis, a favourite source: we might translate it, always something definite is to be undertaken, or put forward. The jottings record also something of his official days: 'they list the number of boys and girls in countless classrooms; they store up problems in geography, history, and arithmetic with which a hard-driven inspector could confront the inspected; they have records of income and expense, down to the last sixpence for a hair-cut.' He had always to be careful, with a family of wife and six children; he certainly drove himself too hard for a poet.

The publication of a brief selection from the Note-Books, by his daughter, Lady Sandhurst, won fresh disciples for Arnold among American writers such as Paul Elmer More and John Livingstone Lowes. These private memoranda bring us nearer to this reserved man: 'they show us much of the journey of his mind and mark a few moments, some of them poignant ones, in his personal history.' Now, on 4 January 1868, 'Little Basil died.' This is followed by several passages from the *Imitation of Christ* to submit himself to the will of God and seek strength there rather than the consolations of man. 'January 11. Dear little Basil was buried. Whosoever shall humble himself as this little child, the same is greatest in the kingdom of Heaven.' This is again followed by citations from the *Imitation*, which he was reading. At the end of the year, 'November 23 – Tommy died. Leva igitur faciem tuam in caelum', again from Thomas à Kempis: Lift thy countenance therefore to heaven. 'November 28 – Tommy's funeral. Awake, thou lute and harp: I myself will awake right early', from the Psalms, followed by various passages from the Bible, and one from a favourite eighteenth-century divine, Bishop Wilson: 'The more you love God, expect you must give the greater proofs of it, and you may expect greater assistance and consolation.' And again: 'The more we deny ourselves the freer we shall be from sin and the more dear to God.' All the same, next year when the anniversary came round: 'November 23 – Tommy!'

In the New Year 1869 he is writing to his mother from Harrow: 'it is a wonderfully clear day, bright with a cold wind, so I went to a field on the top of a hill, whence I can see the clumps of Botleys and the misty line of the Thames, where Tommy lies at the foot of them. I often go for this view on a clear day.' In August he and his wife were again at Laleham. He wrote to his mother, 'it was exactly a year since we have driven there with darling Tommy and the other two boys to see Basil's grave. He enjoyed the drive, and Laleham, and the river, and Matt Buckland's garden, and often talked of them afterwards. And now we went to see *his* grave, poor darling. The two graves are a perfect garden, and are evidently the sight of the churchyard; a path has been trodden over the grass to them by people coming and going. It was a soft, mild air, and we sat a long time by the graves; it is what Flu likes best in the world.' In the Note-Books that summer we read: 'Laleham. My delicate ones have gone rough ways', from the Book of Baruch.

These two boys had been delicate, but in Trevenen Arnold had a son abounding in health and vitality, like himself given to sport and something of an athlete. Yet, while a boy of eighteen at Harrow, he went down with a sudden illness and, within a day or two, was dead. Matt to his mother: 'How fond you were of him, and how I like to recall this! He looks beautiful, and my main feeling about him is, I am glad to say, what I have put in one of my poems, the "Fragment of a Dejaneira":

> *But him, on whom, in the prime*
> *Of life, with vigour undimmed,*
> *With unspent mind, and a soul*
> *Unworn, undebased, undecayed,*
> *Mournfully grating, the gates*
> *Of the city of death have for ever closed –*
> Him, *I count* him *well-starred.'*

In the family Trevenen was known as Budge. We have a glimpse of the boy's character in a letter of Matt to his mother: 'Everything here reminds me of him so much. He made no pretensions about liking flowers or anything else, but he was the one who really cared how the garden was laid out, and kept asking his mamma questions what she was having done about the beds. Then he never passed a morning without giving an eye all round the place, seeing how the animals were getting on, what the gardener was doing, and so on. I do not think we shall stop here beyond Christmas.' He and his wife could not bear to live in their home at Harrow any longer. They thought of moving to Laleham, where 'a vault has been made, and the three brothers are together . . . If Budge had not died I could not have borne to disturb the other two.' Thus to his mother; to himself he cited from the Psalms: 'In the multitude of my thoughts within me thy comforts delight my soul.' Taking refuge, as always at such times, in the *Imitation of Christ*, he prayed for patience in long-suffering.

Next year, 1873, his mother died, full of years, her life singularly fulfilled in her remarkable family, which she had piloted through to their varied and individual achievement. Her own personality and what she had achieved were widely admired. Matt wrote that 'she had a clearness and fairness of mind, an interest in things, and a power of appreciating what might not be in her own line, which were very remarkable, and which remained with her to the very end of her life.' She had written him 'a wonderful letter' about *Literature and Dogma*: 'I can think of no woman in the prime of life, brought up and surrounded as my mother was, and with my mother's sincere personal convictions, who could have written it; and in a woman past eighty it was something astonishing.' Evidently, for all the enclosed orthodoxy of her clerical Penrose upbringing, she had been more open-minded about her son's books than his critics. Dean Stanley wrote: 'what to me was so impressive was not merely that she rose instead of sinking under the blow which we all feared would crush her, but that she retained the life-long reverence for your father's greatness, without a blind attempt to rest in the form and letter of his words.'

For Matt and those who knew his father this would be the end of a period. Dr Arnold was still a living subject of controversy: 'I saw the *Record*: it was like eating its words for the *Record* to put in such a notice after what it had said about Papa. . . . I want to see the *Rock*, which contains, *à propos* of dearest mamma's death, an attack upon Papa.'

We have external glimpses of Matt at this time from his old friend, Judge Coleridge. Trevenen's death had been 'a most bitter and heavy blow', all the worse for being wholly unexpected: 'Forster told me he was terribly cut up by it, but that his behaviour was admirable. He had to be at an examination of pupil teachers, and Mr Forster found him there with his poor eyes full of tears, yet keeping order and

189

doing his duty till he could be relieved.' Coleridge continued to go up and up in the world, now Lord Justice. Matt wrote, with a return to his old spirit of badinage, 'in a few years, if you go on rising and I stagnating, my only right place when I visit you will be, in spite of all your kindness, the servants' hall.'

On the death of Coleridge's father in 1876, Matt wrote: 'from the first time I, as a child, saw him I liked him; which was not the case at all with me so far as all my father's friends were concerned.' Dr Arnold's affection for his Tory friend was carried on in the sons. Three years later Matt returns home late, 'jaded and tired', to read his friend's volume of poems into the dark, 'deeply moved' by the personal ones about Coleridge's dead wife, and warmly commending the translations.

Matt sent him his selections from Wordsworth, with the interesting information that Haydon's portrait, though out of drawing, 'gives more of the real Wordsworth than any other picture I know'. He was pleased that even the *Saturday Review* has now 'fairly given Wordsworth his place as the greatest poet of the last two centuries'. That summer he had been stopping with Coleridge at Heath's Court, and been taken with the line of coast at Sidmouth 'in the misty afternoon light'.

In 1881 Arnold had been in Ireland, equipping himself for the articles he was writing on the subject: 'The Irish press was a new thing to me: it is like the Jacobin press in the heat of the French Revolution. I don't see how Ireland is to settle down while such stimulants to the people's hatred and disaffection are applied every day. But our English pedants will continue to believe in the divine and saving effect, under all circumstances, of right of meeting, right of speaking, right of printing. . . . The temper of Ireland will be neither cowed nor improved.' Arnold must have been staying with Forster as Chief Secretary, whose life was threatened by continual plots. Upon Gladstone's deal with Parnell, the 'Kilmainham Treaty', Forster resigned. His successor was assassinated.

In that year Dean Stanley died. He had been a constant friend to the Arnolds all the way along from his days at Rugby, where he had been a favourite with Dr Arnold – oddly enough, another Celt:

Arthur Penrhyn Stanley, of the fascinating mercurial temperament and irresistible charm. The stolid Anglo-Saxon Doctor must have had a penchant for them, after all, unbeknown to himself. Matt felt it a duty to commemorate Stanley in verse, 'though I am so stupefied with examination papers that I have forgotten that there is such a thing as poetry in the world'. Hence 'Westminster Abbey': 'I was really uncertain, and I am uncertain still, about the public's reception of the poem. I always feel that the public is not disposed to take me cordially; it receives my things, as Gray says it received all his except the "Elegy", with more astonishment than pleasure at first.'

The poem was received with the respect it deserved: no more, for it was not an inspired poem. Arnold thought that Stanley would have been pleased by the use he made of the legend about the appearance of St Peter at the Abbey's foundation. Stanley himself is described:

> Bright wits, and instincts sure,
> And goodness warm, and truth without alloy,
>   And temper sweet, and love of all things pure,
>   And joy in light, and power to spread the joy.

The poem never, at any point, takes wing. How different a case from the poem about the other Arthur, 'Thyrsis'. The reason becomes clear when we read in a later letter, 'I got out to Hinksey and up the hill to within sight of the Cumnor firs. I cannot describe the effect which this landscape always has upon me – the hillside with its valleys, and Oxford in the great Thames valley below.' And again, 'I think Oxford is still, on the whole, the place in the world to which I am most attached.'

It is hardly surprising that in these last years his poems were, each of them, elegiac: those to the two dogs and that to the canary, 'Poor Matthias', are, however, in lighter vein, both tender and amusing: something new in Arnold's verse. The family had moved from Harrow to a cottage, with garden and field, at Cobham among the Surrey hills. His humourless niece, of the portentous Robert Elsmere and Max Beerbohm's cartoon, Mrs Humphry Ward, describes the place: 'the garden beside the Mole, where every bush and flower-bed had its history; and that little study-dressing room . . . not a great multitude of books, but all cherished, all read. No untidiness anywhere; the ordinary litter of an author's room was quite absent.'

She recalls for us the appearance of the two brothers, Matt and Tom, between whom there was only a year's difference in age, who – despite their divergent careers –

> were more alike fundamentally than was often suspected. Both had derived from some remoter ancestry – possibly through their Cornish mother, herself the daughter of a Penrose and a Trevenen – elements and qualities which were lacking in the strong personality of their father. Imagination, 'rebellion against fact', spirituality, a tendency to dream, unworldliness, the passionate love of beauty and charm, 'ineffectualness' in the practical competitive life – these, according to Matthew Arnold, were and are the characteristic marks of the Celt. They were unequally distributed between the two brothers. 'Unworldliness', 'rebellion against fact', 'ineffectualness' in common life, fell rather to my father's share than my uncle's; though my uncle's 'worldliness', of which he was sometimes accused, was never more than skin-deep. Imagination in my father led to a lifelong and mystical preoccupation with religion; it made Matthew Arnold one of the great poets of the 19th century.

Herbert Paul, who knew him, gives us a more objective account of his appearance and personality:

> He was tall, of commanding presence, with black hair which never became grey, and blue eyes. He was short-sighted, and his eye-glass gave him a false air of superciliousness, accentuated by the clever caricaturist of *Vanity Fair*. In reality he was the most genial and amiable of men. But he had a good deal of manner . . . a mixture of old-fashioned courtesy and comic exaggeration. Roughness or rudeness he could not bear. He was essentially a polished man of the world. Considerate politeness to young and old, rich and poor, obscure and eminent, was the practice of his life. . . . His talk was witty, pointed, and often irresistibly droll. Although public speaking did not suit him he had a very flexible voice; he could be very dogmatic in conversation, but

never aggressive or overbearing. For a poet he was surprisingly practical, taking a lively interest in people's incomes, the rent of their houses, the produce of their gardens, the size of their families. He had none of Wordsworth's contempt for gossip, and his father's earnestness had not descended to him.

Archbishop Benson's son has a comment in place here. Someone quoted against the author of *Literature and Dogma* a dictum of his father; Matt was able to reply at last, now older in years than the Doctor at his death, 'Dear Dr Arnold was not infallible.'

For young Mrs Humphry Ward, who had inherited all, and rather more than all, her grandfather's earnestness, the only drawback to visits to Cobham were

the 'dear, dear boys', i.e. the dachshunds, Max and Geist. One would go down to Cobham, eager to talk to Uncle Matt about a book or an article – covetous at any rate of *some* talk with him undisturbed. And it would all end in a breathless chase after Max, through field after field where the little wretch was harrying either sheep or cows, with the dear poet, hoarse with shouting, at his heels. The dogs were always *in the party*, talked to, caressed, or scolded exactly like spoilt children; and the cat of the house was almost equally dear.

One sees that Uncle Matt must have been rather grateful for an excuse to escape.

Geist (Spirit) was Dick's dog, and was given a charming poem on his demise at the age of four.

> *And so there rise these lines of verse*
> *On lips that rarely form them now;*
> *While to each other we rehearse:*
> Such ways, such arts, such looks hadst thou!
>
> *We stroke thy broad brown paws again,*
> *We bid thee to thy vacant chair,*
> *We greet thee by the window-pane,*
> *We hear thy scuffle on the stair.*

We see the flaps of thy large ears
Quick raised to ask which way we go;
Crossing the frozen lake, appears
Thy small black figure on the snow . . .

We lay thee, close within our reach,
Here, where the grass is smooth and warm,
Between the holly and the beech,
Where oft we watched thy couchant form,

Asleep, yet lending half an ear
To travellers on the Portsmouth road –
There build we thee, O guardian dear,
Marked with a stone, thy last abode!

Matthias was the pet canary of his daughter Nelly; if the subject and the measure recall Skelton, the poem has not a little of Gray in its lightness of touch:

Now thy mistress brings thee here,
Says, it fits that I rehearse
Tribute due to thee, a verse,
Meed for daily song of yore
Silent now for evermore.

The other animals are cited, Max and Rover and Great Atossa the cat, who used to eye poor Matthias:

Down she sank amid her fur;
Eyed thee with a soul resigned –
And thou deemedst cats were kind!
– Cruel, but composed and bland,
Dumb, inscrutable and grand,
So Tiberius might have sat,
Had Tiberius been a cat.

Each poem transcends the present with a reflexion beyond the present. Of Geist he wrote:

Stern law of every mortal lot!
Which man, proud man, finds hard to bear,
And builds himself I know not what
Of second life I know not where.

Now –

Birds, companions more unknown,
Live beside us, but alone;
Finding not, do all they can,
Passage from their souls to man.
Kindness we bestow and praise,
Laud their plumage, greet their lays;
Still, beneath their feathered breast,
Stirs a history unexpressed . . .
Proof they give, too, primal powers,
Of a prescience more than ours –
Teach us, while they come and go,
When to sail and when to sow.

Then, the sad thought at end:

We, without thee, little friend,
Many years have not to spend;
What are left, will hardly be
Better than we spent with thee.

Atossa the cat was not commemorated by a poem, but there is a
description of her which shows Arnold very responsive to and
appreciative of the idiosyncratic ways of cats. At Harrow:

> I have just been called to the door by the sweet voice of Tossa,
> whose morning proceedings are wonderful. She sleeps – she has
> just jumped on my lap, and her beautiful tail has made this
> smudge. I was going to say that she sleeps on an armchair before
> the drawing-room fire . . . and enters Flu's room with Eliza
> regularly at half-past seven. Then she comes to my room and
> gives a mew; and then, especially if I let her in and go on writing
> without taking notice of her, there is a real demonstration of
> affection for five minutes such as never again occurs in the day.
> She purrs, she walks round and round me, she jumps in my lap,

she turns to me and rubs her head and nose against my chin; she opens her mouth and raps her pretty white teeth against my pen; then she will jump down, settle herself down by the fire, and never show any more affection all day.

Cats seem to have a built-in sense of time, are routineers in their habits, and apt to be very choosy. We see something of Arnold's domestic interior – up early in the mornings writing away, as he had admonished himself to do on first making jottings in his Note-Books early in married life.

Out of doors there was the pony, Lola, which died early in 1886, while Arnold was away in Germany on his last Commission to report on the respective advantages of fee-paying and free education.

> Your announcement of dear Lola's death [he wrote from Munich] did indeed give me a pang. . . . You have buried her just in the right place, and I shall often stand by the thorn-tree and think of her. I could indeed say, 'Let my last end be like hers!', for her death must have been easy, though I am grieved to hear of her being so wasted and short-breathed. When I was at home at Christmas, I thought she was much as before, and she always liked her apples. . . . There was something in her character which I particularly liked and admired, and I shall never forget her, dear little thing! The tears come into my eyes as I write.

Few people who knew only the rather supercilious exterior of the man of the world could have guessed at the extraordinarily tender heart that lay beneath.

Then there is his last poem, about 'our dear, dear mongrel, Kaiser'. Though the measure is Burns's, the tone is the half-ironic one of Cowper, with a reminiscence of 'John Gilpin' and jesting references to the rival bards of Farringford and Penbryn, Tennyson and the absurd bestseller, the knighted Sir Lewis Morris.

> *What, Kaiser dead? The heavy news*
> *Post-haste to Cobham calls the Muse,*
> *From where in Farringford she brews*
> *The ode sublime,*
> *Or with Penbryn's bold bard pursues*
> *A rival rhyme . . .*

Six years ago I brought him down,
A baby dog, from London town;
Round his small throat of black and brown
 A ribbon blue,
And vouched by glorious renown
 A dachshound true.

His mother, most majestic dame,
Of blood unmixed, from Potsdam came;
And Kaiser's race we deemed the same –
 No lineage higher.
And so he bore the imperial name.
 But ah, his sire!

Kai turned out to be a mongrel, half a collie; but no less lovable for that.

But all those virtues, which commend
The humbler sort who serve and tend,
Were thine in store, thou faithful friend,
 What sense, what cheer!
To us, declining towards our end,
 A mate how dear!

For Max, thy brother-dog, began
To flag, and feel his narrowing span.
And cold, besides, his blue blood ran,
 Since, 'gainst the classes,
He heard, of late, the Grand Old Man [Gladstone]
 Incite the masses.

And so it goes on – how much one prefers it to too much 'high seriousness', and wishes that Arnold had done more, earlier, in this new vein so late attained. For it was his last poem, and his last full year.

He was very much an out-of-doors man, devoted to climbing and walking, and had an extraordinary range of knowledge of flowers. It appears to some extent in his poems, but most of all in his Letters when abroad, with new flowers to observe. Here he is in the Alban

Hills, south of Rome, in 1873. In a wood was 'a feast of flowers. The first I noticed was the dentaria; I think it is the *Dentaria*, a pale lilac flower, with little buttons or teeth; it is rare in England, but grows in a wood near Uxbridge. Then came magnificent butterfly-orchises, then the anemone hepatica, and a white anemone to match it. Then the cyclamen, the purple one, covering all the ground. Then the Star of Bethlehem – but I really cannot go on.' But he did go on, next month, about the woods above the Villa Serbelloni by Lake Como: 'The woods at this season! [May] the lily of the valley everywhere, but not yet perfectly in flower; the helleborine, a beautiful white flower, which we had at Dorking; Solomon's Seal, which I have never seen except in gardens; the dark purple columbine, and the lovely Star of Bethlehem, which fills the same place in the woods and fields now which the grass of Parnassus fills later in the year.'

On his second visit to America there was a whole new botanical range to explore, which fascinated him. In the Berkshire Hills, of Massachusetts, in July 1886,

> on a woody knoll behind this cottage the undergrowth is kalmia, which was all in flower when we came. The *Monotropa uniflora*, (Indian pipe, or corpse-plant, as they call it here – excellent names) is under everywhere, the *Pyrola rotundifolia* in masses. Then we drive out through boggy ground, and towering up everywhere are the great meadow rue, beautifully elegant, the *Helianthus giganteus* and the milkweed – the last (Asclepias) in several varieties and very effective. I believe it is an American plant only, and so I think is the shrubby cinquefoil, which covers waste ground, as the whin does with us. The pokeweed (*Phytolacca*) is, I think, American too, and quite a feature by the wood borders in Pennsylvania. But the great feature in Pennsylvania was the rhododendron by the stream sides and shining in the damp thickets – bushes thirty feet high, covered with white trusses. I was too late for the azalea and for the dogwood. . . . The Cardinal flower I shall see – it is not out yet. A curious thing is our garden golden rod of North England and Scotland, which grows everywhere, like the wild golden rod with us. They have more than thirty kinds of *Solidago*.

It is obvious that Arnold had not only the poet's appreciation of flowers but the botanist's knowledge of them. Friends noticed this on their walks with him in the English countryside; it seems to have been the thing that most aroused his enthusiasm in America.

In 1882 he contemplated retirement, but could not afford it. In 1883 he was taken by surprise by Gladstone's offer of a pension of £250 'as a public recognition of service to the poetry and literature of England'. That was all the *public* recognition he got for his lifetime of hard labour, and he had much scruple about accepting it: 'I should have at once refused, if it were not for those about me.' His wife had been disappointed – as wives are apt to be – at his not getting on better in the world; after all, her father had been a judge. After hesitating for some time he capitulated: 'I was at first in great doubts as to accepting it. However, my official friends were all for accepting, and the public so far seems very kindly disposed about it. Only I hear the *Echo* says I am "a very Bonaparte" for rapacity.'

He had already had a bout with the Income Tax people such as authors are sickeningly familiar with today. His literary returns had been assessed at £1,000 a year, on the ground that his works were mentioned everywhere and must have a wide circulation. Summoned before the Commissioners, ' "You see before you, gentlemen", I said, "what you have often heard of, *an unpopular author.*" The assessment was finally cut down to £200 a year, and I told them I should have to write more articles to prevent my being a loser by submitting to even that assessment. Upon which the Chairman politely said, "Then the public will have reason to be obliged to us." ' They were all gentlemen together dealing with such matters then.

It was in 1885, after his strenuous first American lecture tour, that he had his first warning of the hereditary heart disease which had carried off both Dr Arnold and *his* father in their forties. Matt was now over sixty, and had had a hard life. He was to dine with the Archbishop of Canterbury, 'which I always think a gratifying marvel, considering what things I have published'. But, 'I cannot get rid of the ache across my chest when I walk; imagine my having to stop half a dozen times in going up to Pains Hill! What a mortifying change. But so one draws to one's end.'

However, that autumn he was on the Continent again on his last official Commission, before retirement, to report on free as against fee-paying education. He felt very well, inspecting schools all day in Germany and, in Dresden, going to the theatre every night: 'The schools here are so good that I am never tired of seeing them.' Everywhere he went he met everyone of importance: Mommsen the historian; Baron Tauchnitz, who had made a fortune out of his paperbacks. In Berlin Queen Victoria's daughter, Vicky, the Crown Princess – rather a highbrow – was markedly kind and attentive. 'I am getting to speak German much better than I did at first, but in the "higher circles" almost everyone speaks English, so one does not get practice enough; Prince Bismarck transacts all his business with our Ambassador in English.' What a world away from Bismarck's successor in our time, Adolf Hitler!

Arnold was much taken with Wagner's operas – rather remarkably so for the time, when they were still so much matter of controversy. In Munich he saw *Tristram and Iseult*, adhering to his own title: 'I may say that I have managed the story better than Wagner. The second act is interminable, and without any action.' How much one wishes that Arnold's version of the story had been made the subject of an opera – preferably by Debussy.

In the summer of 1886 he paid his second visit to America – unwise of him in the heat, with his heart-trouble, 'which this climate and its habits do not suit'. His elder daughter, Lucy, had made a happy marriage to a New York lawyer of good family, John Whitridge. A little child of this marriage is buried in the family vault at Laleham. Another child, Arnold Whitridge, very much like his grandfather to look at, has carried on his work in American education in a distinguished career at Yale, and in literature, giving to the public some of his grandfather's unpublished letters and a biography of his great-grandfather, Dr Arnold.

Arnold's mind on this visit was much occupied by the crisis at home over Home Rule. The American papers were all pro-Irish, of course, and he was reported as favourable to Home Rule. He was not – at any rate, not to Gladstone's full measure of it; he was in favour of a graduated scheme progressing onwards from a large measure of local government. Perhaps that was all that could have been achieved, given the balance of forces, at the time. He hoped that the Conservatives and Liberal Unionists, under Salisbury and Hartington, would bring in such a scheme upon Gladstone's defeat. They would not, or could not, take their historic opportunity – and the Irish question went on to poison British politics into this century. Arnold had his answer to American critics who thought that Ulster could be brushed under the carpet without consideration. If local government and devolution come 'to be fairly discussed, the Americans will be capable of seeing that there is no more need for merging Ulster in Southern Ireland than for merging Massachusetts in New York State'.

He did not find America any more interesting than he had before: 'compared with life in England it is so uninteresting, so without savour and without depth.' As for education, '*Das Gemeine* is the American danger; a few and good secondary schools and universities, setting a high standard, are what you seem to me to want, rather than a multitude of institutions which their promoters delude themselves by taking seriously, but which no serious person can so take.' He was more interested in American flowers, of which he was making a list and bringing home specimens.

When he got home to enjoy his retirement, he was kept busier than ever with literary work: 'This summer in America I began to think that my time was really coming to an end, I had so much pain in my chest, the sign of a malady which had suddenly struck down in middle life, long before they came to my present age, both my father and my grandfather.' But he had persevered with his lectures – needs must, to pay his fool of a son's debts. He felt better on returning home. Nevertheless, in the privacy of his Note-Books this year we find: *Il faut entretenir la vigueur du corps pour conserver celle de l'esprit;*[1] and again, *La pensée de la mort nous trompe, car elle nous fait oublier de vivre.*[2] Both of these quotations are from Vauvenargues; he had several times before spurred himself on with this, from Michelet: *Une vie*

---

[1] 'One must keep up one's physical vigour to conserve that of the mind.'
[2] 'The thought of death deceives us, for it makes us forget to live.'

laborieuse, une succession de travaux qui remplissent et moralisent les jours.[1]

He carried the resolution into practice, as always. He reported back to Lucy Whitridge in America, his 'darling child' always: 'I am much pressed with work, but in good spirits, as it is work which is more or less congenial, and not school-inspecting. I have written a preface for the American edition of Mary Claude's stories which you will like; a short preliminary notice for an edition of Wordsworth, a preface for the popular edition of *St Paul and Protestantism*. And now I have to write, rather against time, an article on General Grant's *Life*, of which not 300 copies have been sold in England. That makes it an all the better subject, as there are really materials in the book for a most interesting article, and no-one has used them. Then I have promised a political article for the beginning of the session, and half a dozen pages on Tauler [a theologian], to help a poor ex-colleague who has translated him. There is also Amiel to be done, to fulfil a promise to Mary; so you see I have my hands full.'

This was the translation of Amiel's Journal with which young Mrs Humphry Ward began her literary career – she was to do better with *Robert Elsmere*. She wrote later that she owed both her lifelong interest in French literature and her love of France to her Uncle Matt. Another 'niece' at Oxford – the daughter of Theodore Walrond, one of Matt's oldest friends at Rugby and Oxford – told me that in these last years a messenger, or printer's devil, was often waiting in Uncle Matt's hall for 'copy' from the hard-pressed, now almost popular, writer.

At the end of his letter to Lucy appears the devoted family man, anxious to see his baby grand-daughter: 'how I wish I could go into her room of a morning and hold her little feet while she stares in my face!'

In the privacy of the Note-Books in his last year, 1888, it is still: *Ecce labora et noli contristari,*[2] from St Benedict. From *Ecclesiasticus*, 'Be steadfast in thy covenant, and be conversant therein, and wax old in

---

[1] 'A hard-working life, a succession of labours to fill our days and make them fruitful.'
[2] 'See then, work and be not downcast.'

thy work'; and from Vauvenargues, *Pour exécuter de grandes choses, il faut vivre comme si on ne devais jamais mourir.*[1]

But death was on his way to him. On Sunday, 15 April, he was in Liverpool with his wife to meet their daughter returning from America when he was struck down by a heart-attack in the street, and died.

By a strange presentiment he had written for that day in his Note-Book: 'Weep bitterly over the dead as he is worthy, and then comfort thyself; drive heaviness away: thou shalt not do him good, but hurt thyself.' And, for the Sunday after: 'When the dead is at rest, let his remembrance rest; and be comforted for him when his spirit is departed from him.'

And now they all rest together in the churchyard at Laleham, where he had been born, in the shadow of the redbrick church tower, under the two yews athwart the path. His epitaph, from the Psalms, reads: 'There is sprung up a light for the righteous, and joyful gladness for such as are true hearted.' Fanny Lucy survived him by another thirteen years, to join him in 1901. There with them are their three sons, and the little grandchild, John Whitridge. One reads their epitaphs, none of them doctrinal. For Tommy, his father repeated what he had written in his Note-Books: 'Awake thou, lute and harp; I myself will awake right early'; for Trevenen (their 'Budge'): 'In the morning it is green and groweth up'; for little Basil: 'Suffer little children to come unto me.'

A few early nineteenth-century houses survive nearby, which they would have known; the vicarage occupies the site of Dr Arnold's house; the neighbouring school is now named for his son. Trees and a green shade are all round where they lie, their story over where it all began.

---

[1] 'To achieve great things, one must live as if one should never die.'

Further Reading

The Complete Prose Works of Matthew Arnold, in many volumes, is in course of being published by Michigan University Press (1960–), edited by R. H. Super, who is also editing what we have left of Arnold's correspondence. But it is not necessary to read all of this; the important thing is to read Arnold's best works, the significant ones in his achievement (there is much that is repetitive).

First: the Macmillan edition (1890) of his collected poetry includes the later poems; the Oxford edition (1909) includes his early prize-poems. Most helpful and illuminating is *The Poetry of Matthew Arnold: A Commentary*, by C. B. Tinker and H. F. Lowry (Oxford, 1940). Kenneth Allott's edition in *Longman's Annotated English Poets* (London, 1965) provides poetry and notes conveniently in one volume.

His Letters have been insufficiently appreciated and regarded as unduly reserved; he allowed nothing to survive – outside the poems – that might throw light on his love for Marguerite. But the two volumes edited by G. W. E. Russell (London, 1895; 2nd ed. 1901) give one a full and varied canvas both of his activities and his interests of mind; their only fault is the lack of an index. To these should be added the Letters to A. H. Clough, edited by H. F. Lowry (Oxford, 1932); and Clough's *Correspondence*, edited by F. L. Mulhauser, 2 vols (Oxford, 1957). One wishes that the letters of Arnold's mother might have survived; but we can hope for a good deal of unpublished material when Professor Super's edition of the Letters appears.

Of Arnold's prose-works the principal ones to read are *Essays in Criticism*, first and second series; *Mixed Essays*; *Culture and Anarchy*; *Literature and Dogma*; *The Study of Celtic Literature* (the last is in an Everyman edition).

For education, *A French Eton*, and *Schools and Universities in France*, in one vol. (London, 1892); *Reports on Elementary Schools, 1852–1882*, published in 1889. A valuable commentary is W. F. Connell, *The Educational Thought and Influence of Matthew Arnold* (London, 1950).

On America, *Discourses in America*, and *Civilisation in the United States*; with *Five Uncollected Essays*, edited by Kenneth Allott (Liverpool UP, 1953).

For family background, A. P. Stanley's *Life of Dr Arnold* (first published in 1844, but reissued by Gregg International Publishers in 1970); D. Arnold-Forster, *At War with the Smugglers: Career of Dr Arnold's Father* (London, 1936); F. J. Woodward, *The Doctor's Disciples* (London, 1954). *The Penroses of Fledborough Parsonage: Lives, Letters and Diary*, edited by A. B. Baldwin (Hull, 1933); and *Bibliotheca Cornubiensis* (3 vols, London, 1874, 1882), by G. C. Boase and W. P. Courtney, for the Penroses and Trevenens.

Earlier brief biographies by G. W. E. Russell (London, 1904) and Herbert Paul (London, 1902) have the value that they knew Arnold. There are useful, if academic, studies by Lionel Trilling and Douglas Bush; see also Iris E. Sells' informative *Matthew Arnold and France* (London, 1935), and *Matthew Arnold, the Poetry*, edited by Carl Dawson, in *The Critical Heritage* series (London, 1973).

Photographic Acknowledgments

The Athenaeum 19, 20; Bradford City Art Gallery 23; Elliott and Fry 12; Musée de la Châtre, France 10; National Monuments Record 8, 9; National Portrait Gallery 1, 11; Österreichische Galerie, Vienna 13; Oxford City Library 7, 16, 17, 18; Rugby School 6; Courtesy Messrs Sotheby 15.

Index

Numbers in italics refer to illustrations

Delafield family, New York, 17, 18
Delano family, New York, 156–7
Democracy, 148–9, 150, 160
Denmark, 144–5
Derby, 74
Derby, 14th Earl of, 147
Dickens, Charles, 100, 128, 131
Disraeli B., 97, 133, 147
Dresden, 200

EDUCATION, in Victorian England, 84–8, 117, 127–35
Education Act of 1870, 85, 88, 129–30; of 1902, 9, 123, 135
Elgar, Sir Edward, 153–4
Eliot, T. S., 98, 155–6, 158, 168
Elizabethan Age, 73
Emerson, R. W., 157, 158–9
Erasmus, 140, 174
Ethy, Cornwall, 14, 15, 16, 19
Eton College, 120

FALKLAND, Lord, 176–7
Flaubert, G., 131
Fledborough, Notts., 15–16, 18
Forster, W. E., 71, 85, 88, 123, 124, 129–30, 151–2, 189–90; his wife, see Arnold, Jane
Fox How, Cumbria, 19, 28, 30, 31, 113, 184; 5
France, 32–4, 36, 84, 99, 116–20, 131, 133, 143, 144, 145–6; French Revolution of 1789, 19, 118, 190; of 1848, 184; Second Empire, 36, 118
Frederick the Great, 126
Freeman, E. A., 110
Froude, J. A., 81, 110

GARFIELD, President, 155
Gaulle, Charles de, President, 161
Gell, John, 21, 74
Germany, 99, 100, 111,
117, 118–19, 123, 126, 143, 144–5, 196, 200
Gladstone, W. E., 91, 124, 138, 141, 151–2, 176, 190, 199, 201
Glasgow, 151
Goethe, W., 26, 186
Grant, President, 154, 156, 202
Gray, Thomas, 113, 180
Guiccioli, Countess, 125
Guizot, F., 27, 119

HARDY, Thomas, 70
Harrow, 21, 120, 185, 187, 188
Hawthorne, Nathaniel, 100, 159
Heine, H., 97, 104
Herschel, Sir John, 104
Hesiod, 170
Holland, 85
Homer, 101–4
Hook, Dean, 130
Houghton, Lord, 185
Housman, A. E., 76–7, 102
Hughes, Thomas, 21, 36
Huxley, Thomas, 130, 167
Huxley, Trevenen, 105
Hyde Park, USA, 156

INCOME TAX, 199
India, 11, 82–3, 107
Industrial Revolution, 73
Ipswich, 75
Ireland, 107, 113, 124, 147, 151–3, 171, 190, 200
Italy, 42, 72, 118, 125–6, 198

JAMES, Henry, 33, 154, 155, 160
Jerome, Leonard, 156
Johnson, Dr Samuel, 96
Jowett, Benjamin, 29, 128

KEATS, John, 41, 125
Keble, John, 16, 17, 89
Kempis, Thomas à, 186, 187
Kingsley, Charles, 19, 42

LACORDAIRE, Père, 118, 121
Laleham, 18, 20, 36, 185, 187–8, 203; church, 4
Lansdowne, 3rd Marquis

of, 34, 88, 147; 5th Marquis of, 158
Larkin, Philip, 75
Leavis, F. R., 98
Lewes, G. H., 96
Lewis, C. S., 98, 165
Liberal Party, 135, 138, 152, 174–5
Lincoln, President, 154
Lingen, Lord, 85, 124
Liverpool, 128, 203
Lloyd George, D., 111
London, 35–8, 72, 74, 105, 116, 183; elementary schools, 86; university, 128; University Hall, 72
Lowe, Robert, 85, 87–8
Lowestoft, 16–17
Luther, Martin, 110
Lytton, Lord, 128–9

MACAULAY, Lord, 178
Manchester, 72, 128
Manning, Cardinal, 165, 171
Markham, Mrs, 16
Marx, Karl, 186; Marxism, 173
Mathilde, Princess, 125
Mauritius, 124
Melville, Herman, 162
Mérimée P., 118
Miall, Edward, 84, 85, 126, 129
Middle classes, 122, 131–5, 139–41, 144–5
Mill, J. S., 10, 129, 167
Morant, Sir Robert, 117
Morley, Lord, 129, 174–5
Morris, Sir Lewis, 196
Müller, Max, 28
Musset, Alfred de, 104

NAPOLEON III, 118
Nehru, Pandit, 107
New York, 17, 35, 156, 165
New Zealand, 21
Niebuhr, B. G., 11, 18
Noetics, the Oxford, 17
Nohant, France, 33
Nonconformity, 84, 85, 117, 120, 129–30, 141, 152, 164, 173

'OBERMANN' (E. Senancour), 38, 41, 46, 91